WOMEN OF CHARACTER

ONE MINUTE BIBLE

90 Refreshing Readings on Courage and Virtue

LAWRENCE KIMBROUGH

BROADMAN
&HOLMAN
PUBLISHERS

Nashville, Tennessee

Contents

Introduction

When we see the end result of godly character in others' lives, we're awed by it. We tell our friends about it. We want it.

But how badly do we want it? I ask this (of you, and of myself) because genuine character is most often grown on overcast afternoons, in the early mornings before anyone else is awake, on days when we'd rather be doing just about anything besides what's in front of us.

The Marys and Marthas of the Bible understood this. So did the Esthers and Elizabeths. They let their faith in God drive them farther into the deep end than they ever thought possible . . . and found the only place where the swimming is really worthwhile.

My, what we can learn from them!

And in God's curious way of communicating, we can even learn from the likes of Jezebel and Job's wife—ladies who lacked the desire to do any better, yet still remind us what we all could become if left to our own demands and devices.

I hope this careful, honest look at the women of the Bible—both the weak and the strong—will meet you in the middle of your mornings, your evenings, your everyday life . . . and give you good reason again to want it really bad.

Whatever was written before was written for our instruction,
so that through our endurance and through the encouragement
of the Scriptures we may have hope.

Romans 15:4

Eve
DECEIVED

When we look into Eve's eyes, we see our own. We can all attest to times when we were walking in the Spirit one minute and walking in the flesh the next. That's how quickly temptation can trip us up. That's how easily we can all be deceived.

The woman said to the serpent, "We may eat the fruit from the trees in the garden. But about the fruit of the tree in the middle of the garden, God said, 'You must not eat it or touch it, or you will die.' "

"No! You will not die," the serpent said to the woman. "In fact, God knows that when you eat it your eyes will be opened and you will be like God, knowing good and evil."

Then the woman saw that the tree was good for food and delightful to look at, and that it was desirable for obtaining wisdom. So she took some of its fruit and ate it.

There comes a point when the devil has already tried most of the temptations he's going to throw at us. Then he primarily just repeats the ones that work. That's why one of our best weapons is knowing when he's likely to strike and what tool he's likely to use. So don't be surprised to hear from him when you're lonely, depressed, overworked, unappreciated. Those are his signals that you're ripe to be picked by an old, familiar habit. But let temptations be *your* signals, too—to be ready, to be on guard.

Look At It This Way

How tragic to view God's children caught in this vicious trap, eagerly seeking something better than God's best. Adam and Eve were living in paradise — no difficulties, no trials, no sorrows. They had perfect fellowship, perfect intimacy, perfect harmony. Yet Satan convinced them that he could offer something better. That "something better" turned out to be adding toil to work, attaching pain to childbirth, and introducing murder to the family circle. Likewise, every sin is a senseless and superstitious belief in the supposedly beneficial effects of sin.

Ultimately, this is the end of temptation's path. Prompted by human desire to be independent of God and to overcome obstacles with a determination to assert one's own rights, we are willing to doubt God's goodness (we even consider his protective goodness a hindering restriction). We refuse to believe his promises of happiness and fruitfulness as rewards for obedience. And we covet his preeminent holiness for ourselves, wanting to make our own decisions and enthroning ourselves as equal to God himself.

—*Dorothy Kelley Patterson*

YOU'D THINK AFTER LOSING TO HIM SO MANY TIMES, WE'D REALIZE WE'RE NO MATCH FOR SATAN. CALL OUT TO JESUS AT THE FIRST HINT OF TEMP-TATION. THE DEVIL KNOWS WHO'S BOSS.

Noah's Wife
STANDING BY HER MAN

Noah's wife never dreamed what marriage would cost, primarily the pleasant anonymity of being just another normal member of society. No, everyone would know who Noah's wife was . . . though she wouldn't know it herself until she'd lived her commitment.

In the six hundredth year of Noah's life, in the second month, on the seventeenth day of the month, on that day all the sources of the watery depths burst open, the floodgates of the sky were opened, and the rain fell on the earth 40 days and 40 nights.

On that same day Noah along with his sons Shem, Ham, and Japheth, Noah's wife, and his three sons' wives entered the ark with him. . . . Two of all flesh that has the breath of life in it entered the ark with Noah. Those that entered, male and female of all flesh, entered just as God had commanded him. Then the LORD shut him in.

Whenever you're in the middle of a marriage problem (or *any* problem)—when you're so mad you don't know what to do, so hurt you can't believe what you're thinking—when you're trying to decide how to respond, make yourself finish the following sentence: "I can look back later at what I did and say . . ." That you quit? Or that you stuck it out, you swallowed your pride, you made yourself forgive, you kept your promise. Problems look so much bigger on the inside. Pull back, and see them in a different light.

Look At It This Way

Can you imagine what Mrs. Noah must have thought when her husband said that a great flood was coming to their arid region, and their only means of survival would be trusting God and building an ark? Can you imagine the sons trying to convince their wives of the same? What kind of family commitment did it take for Mrs. Noah—and especially for the sons and their wives—to support Mr. Noah in this faith venture? Remember, the ridicule lasted for about a century of ark construction before the first drop of rain ever fell. Now that's commitment!

Life brings its crises—traumatic illness, death of a loved one, loss of a job. A crisis can tear a family apart or knit it more closely together. A family that upholds each other in a time of crisis can turn a crisis into a life challenge they face and handle together—with God's help. There is nothing like the support of a loving family in offering counsel, solutions, and encouragement.

Noah's truly was the model family—the only family on earth that God chose to preserve. They must have been an incredible bunch.

—Jim Henry

IF A 100-YEAR BOAT PROJECT ISN'T GROUNDS FOR DIVORCE, THEN WHAT ABOUT THE PROBLEMS YOU'RE HAVING? NO, MARRIAGE ISN'T EASY, BUT MARRIAGE IS FOREVER. BE THERE TO SEE IT THROUGH.

Sarah
PASSING THE BLAME

Selections from Genesis 16

Let it be of some comfort to you to know that the father and mother of nations found themselves at odds with each other enough times in their marriage that one of their big fights even made its way into the Bible for all the world to see. The rest is history.

Abram's wife Sarai had not borne him children. She owned an Egyptian slave named Hagar. Sarai said to Abram, "Since the LORD has prevented me from bearing children, go to my slave; perhaps I can have children by her.". . . He slept with Hagar, and she became pregnant.

When she realized that she was pregnant, she looked down on her mistress. Then Sarai said to Abram, "You are responsible for my suffering! I put my slave in your arms, and ever since she saw that she was pregnant, she has looked down on me.". . . Then Sarai mistreated her so much that she ran away from her.

Sarah was definitely out of line to tear into her husband like this, especially after seeming to be the brains behind the whole Hagar arrangement to begin with. But still, Abraham was the man of the house, and he certainly didn't have to go along with the idea. The fact is, both of them were hunting a logical, human way around God's elusive promise; and in their mutual impatience, they got themselves into marital hot water. When we fall out of submission to God, there's no way we can submit to each other.

Look At It This Way

Have you noticed lately that everyone seems to be a victim? We will leave it to the social commentators to explain just how our new culture of victimization will affect society, but we know exactly how it can affect a marriage. Once a husband or wife becomes wrapped up in the blame game (blaming parents, genes, a boss, or a spouse), a vicious cycle of shirked responsibility permeates the relationship. Soon each partner is looking for ways to avoid responsibility and shift the blame. Of course, this is nothing new. Ever since Adam blamed Eve, and Eve blamed the serpent, we have learned the trick of finding excuses.

As human beings with a free will, we have choices and nobody makes them for us. While we are not necessarily the cause of all that happens in our lives, we are responsible for what we make of what happens. Don't let your marriage become a blame game. Don't lay the blame on your church, your parents, your schooling, your income, your siblings, your friends, or anything else. Take responsibility for your feelings and your actions, and watch your marriage mature.

—*Les and Leslie Parrott*

BEING QUICK TO JUDGE CAN CAUSE SOME HURTFUL WORDS TO ESCAPE INTO OUR MARRIAGES —AND WE ALL KNOW HOW HARD THEY ARE TO RETRIEVE. BE SLOW TO SPEAK, EVEN SLOWER TO ASSIGN BLAME.

Sarah
LAUGHING ON THE PROMISES

Selections from Genesis 18

Sarah's story is a reminder that God can still find something to work with in our doubt and disbelief, moving us past our point of comfort and control. He's the kind of God who's willing to tolerate Sarah's snickering and still let her have the last laugh.

The LORD appeared to Abraham at the oaks of Mamre. . . . He looked up, and he saw three men standing near him. . . . "Where is your wife Sarah?" they asked him. "There, in the tent," he answered. The LORD said, "I will certainly come back to you in about a year's time, and your wife Sarah will have a son!"

Now Sarah was listening at the entrance of the tent behind him. . . . So she laughed to herself: "After I have become shriveled up and my lord is old, will I have delight?" But the LORD asked Abraham, "Why did Sarah laugh, saying, 'Can I really have a baby when I'm old?' Is anything impossible for the LORD?"

We get another swell picture of Sarah's character over in Genesis 21, after Isaac has been born and Sarah has had a chance to reflect on the impossibility that's now cooing in her arms. "God has made me laugh," she said, looking dreamily into the eyes of her little one—the one whose name actually does mean *laughter*—"and everyone who hears will laugh with me." She wasn't afraid to reflect on her failures. They made God's faithfulness shine even brighter. Funny how that works, isn't it?

Look At It This Way

When God speaks, what he asks of us requires faith. Our major problem, however, is our self-centeredness. We think we have to accomplish the assignment on our own power and with our current resources.

We forget that when God speaks, he always reveals what he is going to do—not what he wants us to do for him. We join him so he can do his work through us. We don't have to be able to accomplish the task within our limited ability or resources. With faith we can proceed confidently, because we know that he is going to bring to pass what he purposes.

When God invites you to be involved with him, he is wanting to reveal himself to you and to a watching world. Therefore, he will ask you to be involved with him in a God-sized assignment. When you are confronted with such a great assignment, you will face a crisis of belief. You will have to decide what you really believe about the God who called you. And how you respond to God will reveal what you believe about him regardless of what you say.

—Henry Blackaby

JUST BECAUSE YOU'VE MADE SOME MISTAKES DOESN'T MEAN GOD IS THROUGH WITH YOU. DRAW NEAR TO HIM TODAY. MAYBE THE TWO OF YOU CAN HAVE A BIG LAUGH ABOUT HOW SILLY YOU'VE BEEN.

Sarah

INNER BEAUTY

Selections from 1 Peter 3

We can get a rather one-sided picture of Sarah. All we remember is that little laughing episode. But her legacy outlived her laughter. In her we see a person who—like us—was obviously far from perfect, yet still could catch the eye of God.

Submit yourselves to your own husbands so that, even if some disobey the Christian message, they may be won over without a message by the way their wives live, when they observe your pure, reverent lives.

Your beauty should not consist of outward things . . . instead, it should consist of the hidden person of the heart with the imperishable quality of a gentle and quiet spirit, which is very valuable in God's eyes. For in the past, the holy women who hoped in God also beautified themselves in this way, submitting to their own husbands, just as Sarah obeyed Abraham.

"*Y*ou are [Sarah's] daughters if you do what is right and do not give way to fear" (1 Peter 3:6, NIV). Fear? Is that what it is? Is it some form of fear that convinces us we need to hide behind the masks of a perfect face, a perfect home, a perfect family? And since we know that perfect love truly does cast out fear, can we perhaps blame our desire to present a polished front on the fact that we don't love ourselves the way we should—the way God loves us, with a blind, unconditional love that sees past our imperfections?

Look At It This Way

The churches who first received Peter's message probably reflected the social divisions that prevailed throughout the Roman world. One or two percent of the population was far wealthier than the average woman ever dreamed of being. In the church, which was not yet fashionable, there were probably just a few well-to-do women. However, they were expected to be walking advertisements of their men's wealth and status. Carefully coiffed hair peeked from under demure veils, fabrics were the very best, and jewelry glittered everywhere.

The purpose of all this finery was less to allure men than to compete with the other rich women. But in the church, these distinctions had undermined the goal of bonding women together as sisters in Christ. Peter had no patience with rich men who wanted to use their wives as status emblems, nor with rich women who wanted to lord it over the poor. He urged women to lay aside their trappings of wealth as a spiritual discipline to train themselves in humility —an outward sign that they considered the other women their full equals.

—*Karen Lee-Thorp and Cynthia Hicks*

WOULDN'T IT BE GREAT IF WE COULD LET GOD HAVE CONTROL OF EVEN THE UNSEEN SIDE OF OUR LIVES, SO THAT IF THE WHOLE WORLD KNEW EVERY-THING ABOUT US—WARTS AND ALL—THAT'D BE ALL RIGHT?

Lot's Wife
TURNING BACK

Her home, her friends, all the life she had known for years was melting in an acid bath—right at her backside. Who of us could've kept from glancing over our shoulder? But God knew that she was not turning her head in horror, but in homesickness.

At the crack of dawn the angels urged Lot on: "Get up! Take your wife and your two daughters who are here, or you will be swept away in the punishment of the city." But he hesitated, so because of the LORD's compassion for him, the men grabbed his hand, his wife's hand, and the hands of his two daughters. And they brought him out and left him outside the city. . . .

Then the LORD rained burning sulfur on Sodom and Gomorrah out of the sky. He overthrew these cities, the entire plain, all the inhabitants of the cities, and whatever grew on the ground. But his wife looked back and became a pillar of salt.

Look back at all that God had done to spare this family from dying in Sodom's demise. He had first given them an exemption, thanks to Abraham's prayers. He had sent angels right to their door to escort them to the city limits. The messengers had practically dragged them from their home, and even consented for them to stop short of their intended destination when Lot's legs got tired and the shock set in. Yet all God's help wasn't enough for his wife. How could such a powerful, personal love not hold her attention?

Look At It This Way

A voice said, *Climb.* And he said, "How shall I climb? The mountains are so steep that I cannot climb."

The voice said, *Climb or die.* He said, "But how? I see no way up those steep ascents. This that is asked of me is too hard for me."

Then he remembered that he had read in the books of the bravest climbers on the hills of earth, that sometimes they were aware of the presence of a Companion on the mountains who was not one of the earthly party of climbers. How much more certain was the presence of his Guide as he climbed the high places of the spirit. And he remembered a word that heartened him: "My soul is continually in my hand" (Psalm 119:109, KJV). It heartened him, for it told him that he was created to walk in precarious places, not on the easy levels of life. And he said to his foe, Love-of-Fleshly-Ease, "Rejoice not against me, O mine enemy: when I fall, I shall arise; when I sit in darkness, the Lord shall be a light unto me" (Micah 7:8, KJV).

And he said, "I will climb."

—Amy Carmichael

ARE YOU FRUSTRATED, OFTEN FAILING THE LORD, YET UNABLE TO GIVE UP THE HABITS AND RELATIONSHIPS THAT CONTINUE DRAGGING YOU UNDER? TURN YOUR BACK ON THE THINGS THAT TURN YOU AWAY.

Hagar

OVERWHELMED BY WORRY

Hagar is one of the more tragic figures of the Bible. Brought in without her asking to an impatient situation—to add an element of logic to God's impossible promise—she simply did as she was told, only to find herself rejected and alone.

Abraham got up, took bread and a waterskin, put them on Hagar's shoulders, and sent her and the boy away. . . . When the water in the skin was gone, she left the boy under one of the bushes. Then she went and sat down nearby, about a bowshot away, for she said, "I can't bear to watch the boy die!". . .

God heard the voice of the boy, and the angel of God called to Hagar from heaven and said to her, "What's wrong, Hagar? Don't be afraid, for God has heard the voice of the boy from the place where he is. Get up, help the boy up, and sustain him, for I will make him a great nation."

"Lord, what else am I supposed to do but worry when my son was due in by midnight and it's now 2:45, or my two-year-old splits her chin on the garage floor? Isn't that stuff worth worrying about?" Sure it is. But God wants you to realize that he is tending to your needs—not just when your helplessness is thick and tangible—but even in those times when you feel the most in control. Remembering that you are never outside of his care will help you worry less in moments when it just feels like you are.

Look At It This Way

"I'd never been a fearful person or felt vulnerable until I had children," says Deena, a mother of three. But that changed when her infant daughter Caitlin's lungs burst due to pulmonary hypertension, and she had to be airlifted to a Houston hospital in critical condition. At that point, Deena realized how little control she had and was able to entrust her baby's medical problems to God's care. But when she got Caitlin home after many weeks in the hospital, this young mother found herself protective and clingy.

When fear and worry gripped her, Deena made a habit of sitting down and jotting on paper all God's past goodness in their lives. "I remind myself they're God's children, and I'm more a caretaker than an owner. He's their heavenly Father, the one who created them and promises he'll work everything in their lives for a pattern of good. And then I think of the many answered prayers, how Caitlin recovered, of the blessings that came out of difficult times." Then she's freer to open her hands and heart, lay her children and their problems before God, and experience his comforting presence.

—*Cheri Fuller*

WORRY HAS A SOMEWHAT HEALTHY SIDE THAT CAN MOTIVATE US TO ACTION, BUT IT TENDS TO HANG AROUND LONG AFTER, DRIVING OUR FAITH INTO FEAR. LEARN TO DISCERN WHEN WORRY HAS CROSSED THE LINE.

Rebekah
A SERVANT'S HEART

Selections from Genesis 24

---

*She had no
idea who was
approaching
her that hot,
thirsty after-
noon, or that
such a chance
encounter
would change
her life forever.
But you never
know what
kind of oppor-
tunities will
arise when
you start with
a servant's
heart.*

"Let the girl to whom I say, 'Please lower your water jug so that I may drink,' and who responds, 'Drink, and I'll water your camels also'—let her be the one You have appointed for Your servant Isaac.". . .

Before he had finished speaking, there was Rebekah. . . . Then the servant ran to meet her and said, "Please let me have a little water from your jug." She replied, "Drink, my lord." She quickly lowered her jug to her hand and gave him a drink. When she had finished giving him a drink, she said, "I'll also draw water for your camels until they have had enough to drink."

You know those times when someone seems to pop into your mind out of nowhere? You tell yourself you should give her a call, jot her a note, ask her to lunch. Or maybe it's not a particular person but a ministry area that you continue to sense God drawing you to. Who's to say, as Rebekah discovered, that God isn't prompting you for service out of response to someone's prayers? Try making sure you follow up on those uncanny occurrences. They seem like nothing, but only eternity can measure their significance.

Look At It This Way

My heart's desire is to find more opportunities to give myself away and teach my children the joy of service at the same time. One little problem, though: When?! A friend of mine once moaned, "There's just not enough of me to go around."

Lots of us feel the same way and can't bear the thought of adding one more activity, one more to-do item to our list, however worthy it may be. For busy women like us, who don't know how we could manage the added role of being a volunteer, psychologist Virginia O'Leary offers a word of encouragement: "The more roles women have, the better off they are, and the less likely they are to be depressed or discouraged about their lives. When we have a lot to do, we complain that it's driving us crazy—but, in fact, it's what keeps us sane."

It's ironic that one of the best remedies for impending burnout is to give yourself away—to pick out one time and place each week where you can stretch out your hands for the pure joy of doing it.

—*Liz Curtis Higgs*

YOU ONLY HAVE SO MUCH TIME TO SHARE. BUT IF GOD KNOWS YOU'RE WILLING TO FOLLOW HIS LEADING, HE'LL HELP YOU MAKE THE MOST OF THE TIME YOU HAVE. OFFER HIM A SERVANT'S HEART.

Rebekah
MASTER OF MANIPULATION

Selections from Genesis 27

---

*Tricking
Isaac to make
him honor
Jacob over
their older son
didn't just
pop into their
mother's head
overnight. No,
she'd been
watching,
plotting,
strategizing.
Wonder what
might have
happened if
she'd have put
that much
effort into her
marriage?*

While Esau went to the field to hunt some game to bring in, Rebekah said to her son Jacob, "Listen! I heard your father talking with your brother Esau. . . . Now obey every order I give you, my son. Go to the flock and bring me two choice young goats, and I will make them into a delicious meal for your father—the kind he loves. Then take it to your father to eat so that he may bless you before he dies."

Jacob answered . . . "Then I will seem to be deceiving him, and I will bring a curse rather than a blessing on myself." His mother said to him, "Your curse be on me, my son."

Remember the Rebekah we met back in Genesis 24? The sweet little Hebrew girl who went out of her way to serve Abraham's messenger, drawing up enough buckets to cool off all ten of his camels? (And, boy, can they drink a lot!) Look at her now. Just goes to show you what can happen when we leave our marriages unattended, unfed, uncultivated. People who once pledged their love at the altar can become strangers living in the same house. What are you doing to keep that from happening at your house?

Look At It This Way

This may have been the culmination of a long-term power struggle. Both Isaac and Rebekah may have been resorting to that age-old tactic we call passive-aggressive behavior. In short, they were giving each other the silent treatment. Whatever the dynamic in this relationship, Rebekah determined she had to help God fulfill the prophecy he gave her regarding Jacob. He must have Isaac's blessing in order to "be stronger than" Esau. Unfortunately, she forgot that God had decreed that "the older will serve the younger." What God predetermines, he will bring to pass, though he chooses to use human beings to carry out his purposes. He never decrees that people use deceptive and manipulative methods to help him accomplish his divine plans. Very seldom does God condone the end justifying the means. He is a God of truth and light, and "in him there is no darkness at all" (1 John 1:5, NIV). What Rebekah did was clearly wrong. She was a bad example and a stumbling block for her son Jacob, and she dishonored her husband with her forthright and deliberate deception.

—*Gene Getz*

THERE ARE LOTS OF WAYS TO BE DECEITFUL IN MARRIAGE. WE MAY CALL IT BEING "LESS THAN TRUTHFUL," BUT THAT'S JUST A NICE WAY TO SAY WE'RE LYING, MANIPULATING, CONTROLLING. IS THAT PERSON YOU?

Leah
REJECTED YET FAITHFUL

Selections from Genesis 29

If ever a marriage got off on the wrong foot, it was Jacob and Leah's. The look in his eyes wasn't the warm glow of wedded bliss but the bitter glares of betrayal. Yet Leah learned that what God thinks of you is the most important reflection of who you are.

When the LORD saw that Leah was unloved, He opened her womb; but Rachel was barren. Leah conceived, gave birth to a son, and named him Reuben, for she said, "The LORD has seen my affliction; surely my husband will love me now."

She conceived again, gave birth to a son, and said, "The LORD heard that I am unloved and has given me this son also.". . . She conceived again, gave birth to a son, and said, "At last, my husband will become attached to me because I have borne him three sons.". . . And she conceived again, gave birth to a son, and said, "This time I will praise the LORD."

*N*o, it's not too much to ask of your husband that your relationship become a priority to him—not always taking a back seat to work, hobbies, and whatever it is that keeps his mind so preoccupied. But it is too much to *demand*. Nothing in your scolding is likely to change his mind or to melt the hard shell on his icy, detached habits. If you want to get his attention, honor him. Serve him. Love him. Make the brave decision that you will do what's right even when your husband does you wrong.

Look At It This Way

There's a fundamental problem with expecting fulfillment from people, places, and things. These are the gifts of life, not the source of life. Anytime we expect the gifts of life to give us what only God can, we're asking for our cups to be drained of energy and life itself.

When I focus on Jesus Christ as the source of my life, an amazing thing happens. Because he loves me and actually possesses the wisdom, love, peace, and joy I've always wanted—he alone can fill my cup to overflowing! Because I'm no longer expecting people to fill my cup, I'm not hurt when they don't respond in a particular way. Psalm 62 says that we are to wait and hope in God alone. He's our rock, our salvation, our rear guard, our hiding place. He's everything we'll ever need!

The more we place our expectations on another person, the more control we give them over our emotional and spiritual state. The freer we are of expectations from others—and the more we depend upon God alone—the more pure and honest our love for others will become.

—*Gary Smalley*

REJECTION IS NOT DEFEATED BY MORE REJECTION BUT BY THE REVERSE—BY UNCONDITIONAL ACCEPTANCE THAT LOOKS INTO THE FACE OF DISAPPROVAL AND SEES A HURTING PERSON WHO NEEDS YOUR LOVE.

Rachel
CHILDLESS

Selections from Genesis 29 & 30

The difficult dynamics of polygamy had to have been murder on everyone— even in the very best of circumstances. Imagine how thick the tension became when only one of the wives— the homely one—was able to have any children. This is not going to be pretty.

Laban had two daughters: the older was named Leah, and the younger was named Rachel. Leah had delicate eyes, but Rachel was shapely and beautiful. Jacob loved Rachel. . . .

When Rachel saw that she was not bearing Jacob any children, she envied her sister. "Give me sons, or I will die!" she said to Jacob. Jacob became angry with Rachel and said, "Am I in God's place, who has withheld children from you?". . .

Then God remembered Rachel. He listened to her and opened her womb. She conceived and bore a son, and said, "God has taken away my shame."

Rachel responded as a lot of us do when we feel the pinch of a big problem. Seeing no way out, weary of waiting on God to answer in her time frame, desperation overpowered her faith and trust and forced her into making foolish decisions—blaming her husband, wishing she was dead, grasping at a quick-fix solution. As maddening or frustrating as our own particular trials may be, we never make them any better by letting our emotions outrun our confidence in God. We can only proceed with prayer.

Look At It This Way

Nothing else in my life has been as baffling to me as not being able to conceive a child. My heart cries out to the Lord, "Why will You not do this simple thing for me? You do it for so many so easily. You give children to those who will never teach them about Your marvelous grace. Why not me?"

He does not, as so many do, tell me that "my time will come" . . . that if I will just relax and not try so hard, everything will be okay . . . that "If you adopt a baby, you'll get pregnant." He does say that he is with me. He weeps with me as Jesus wept for Lazarus. He reminds me that he is good and that he can be trusted with my heart. Any doubt of that was wiped away at the cross.

He has given his best to me, his own beautiful, beloved child. Will he withhold any good thing from me? No, never. Is Jesus enough to make up for this aching void in my soul? I do not always feel that it is so. But it is. Jesus loves me—this I know.

—*Debbie Trickett*

WHEN OUR TROUBLES ARE TOTALLY BEYOND OUR CONTROL— SUCH AS INFERTILITY—THE ONLY SURE RESTING PLACE IS IN THE GOODNESS OF GOD. IF YOU CAN BELIEVE HE KNOWS BEST, YOU CAN HANDLE ANYTHING.

Rachel & Leah
LEAVING AND CLEAVING

Selections from Genesis 31

Jacob had Rachel and Leah called to the field where his flocks were. He said to them, "I can see from your father's face that his attitude toward me is not the same, but the God of my father has been with me. . . . And He said . . . 'Get up, leave this land, and return to your native land.' "

Rachel and Leah answered him, "Do we have any portion or inheritance in our father's household? Are we not regarded by him as outsiders? For he has sold us and has certainly spent our money. In fact, all the wealth that God has taken from our father belongs to us and to our children. So do whatever God has said to you."

How do you manage to preserve your allegiance to your spouse and obey the commandment of honoring your parents at the same time—when doing one feels like you're forsaking the other? The short answer has to be this: When forced to choose, you must give preference to your husband, your children, and your family over your mom and dad. But you can still honor your parents in the way you say no, by making sure to be clear and up-front about how your grown-up relationship with them is needing to travel.

Look At It This Way

As I teeter on the brink of the possibility of one of our children meeting the person he or she will marry, I find myself feeling both jittery and excited. I know the intimacy of their relationship will close me out of part of my closeness to my child, as it should. It will mean yet another transition.

God tells our young people to leave their fathers and mothers and cleave to their spouses in marriage. As parents, we must honor their attempts to do so by allowing them to put their mates first. Along with the marriage license usually come keys to a house or an apartment that means our home is no longer their primary home. Along with the wedding bells comes the end of the expectation that they will be home for Christmas.

Admittedly, this part of the journey is a bit frightening to me, but most who have gone before me assure me that marriage enlarges the circle of a family. So I trust God that when we get to the wedding bells part, He will provide the same adaptive attitude and strength that have sustained me each step of the way.

—*Carol Kuykendall*

THE BREAK FROM HOME IS HARDER ON SOME THAN ON OTHERS. BUT THE LONG-TERM EFFECTS OF ALLOWING HEAVY DOSES OF PARENTAL INTRUSION INTO YOUR MARRIAGE IS A MUCH HARDER PILL TO SWALLOW.

Jochebed
PROTECTING HER HERITAGE

Selections from Exodus 2

She's remembered for her quiet rebellion against Pharaoh's bloody decree. But she'd probably tell you she didn't think twice about it. Taking her best shot at preserving her son Moses' life was her only real choice.

A man from the family of Levi married a Levite woman. The woman became pregnant and gave birth to a son; when she saw that he was beautiful, she hid him for three months. But when she could no longer hide him, she got a papyrus basket for him and coated it with asphalt and pitch. She placed the child in it and set it among the reeds by the bank of the Nile. . . .

Pharaoh's daughter went down to bathe at the Nile while her servant girls walked along the riverbank. Seeing the basket among the reeds, she sent her slave girl to get it. When she opened it, she saw the child—a little boy, crying.

You never know what those little children who call your house home are going to grow up to do. But like Jochebed, you will at some point have to float their potential out on the water, release them from your control, and entrust them into the hands that loaned them to you in the first place. Make sure you've prepared them well. Make sure they know who their God is. Make sure their faith is given plenty of room to grow, so that whatever they end up doing, they'll do it in his strength.

Look At It This Way

Fifty years ago, Joseph Stalin decided to destroy the Lutheran church in Russia. The Lutherans were to be a case study in how all the Christian denominations might eventually be liquidated. First, Stalin had the pastors killed or imprisoned. Then the church buildings were confiscated. Lutheran families were broken up. Men were forced into the army. Women and children were loaded into boxcars like cattle and scattered throughout the remote regions of the Soviet Union. In a shockingly brief time, the Lutheran Church of the Soviet Union was wiped off the face of the earth.

But that's not the end of the story.

The Lutheran women worked stubbornly, painfully, to keep the church alive. They sought each other out across miles of desolate countryside. They met in one another's homes. They wrote down all the religious instruction they had learned by heart. And at the risk of imprisonment, they passed on the faith to their children. The Lutheran church was reborn. It now meets in more than five hundred house churches. The church has outlasted Communism.

—Charles Colson

PRAY THAT GOD WOULD REVEAL TO YOU ENOUGH OF WHAT HE HAS IN MIND FOR YOUR KIDS THAT YOU CAN SHAPE THEM WELL FOR THE FUTURE. TRUST HIM TO USE YOU IN WAYS YOU MAY NOT YET REALIZE.

Miriam
ALIVE WITH WORSHIP

Selections from Exodus 14 & 15

The Red Sea resumed its steady coursing, the shrieks of Egypt's bravest succumbing to its undertow. And on the far banks of safety stood hundreds of thousands—dead if not for the strong, saving arm of God. And alive with worship.

The Israelites had walked through the sea on dry ground, with the waters like a wall to them on their right and their left. That day the LORD saved Israel from the power of the Egyptians, and Israel saw the Egyptians dead on the seashore. When Israel saw the great power that the LORD used against the Egyptians, the people feared the LORD and believed in Him. . . .

Then Miriam the prophetess, Aaron's sister, took a tambourine in her hand, and all the women followed her. . . . Miriam sang to them: "Sing to the LORD, for He is highly exalted; He has thrown the horse and its rider into the sea."

When will we understand that worship is so much more than Sunday morning? Worship is a prayer of thanksgiving that dances off the rolled-up windows of our cars. Worship is knowing we should get inside and go to bed, if only we could tear ourselves away from this dazzling nighttime sky. Worship is praising God for the sobbing teenage daughter in our arms, knowing she didn't really mean what she said to us this morning. There's not a single situation we'll face this week that won't be worthy of worship.

Look At It This Way

[MIRIAM:] Unless you have experienced the bitterness of captivity, you cannot imagine how sweet freedom tastes. Beside those waters of deliverance, I danced. There on the edge of the waiting wilderness, I simply allowed my heart its freedom.

I danced because I had to dance. I danced to offer God my little faith, which had been held captive by my doubt. I broke my chains of fear with my joyous movement.

Now we face a long journey. Where will this God of surprises lead us? I shall continue to sing into the wind. I will lead others in the dance of the desert. On long, dry days when my people cannot remember the songs of their hearts, I will sing the songs for them. I shall remember the waters of my own deliverance. I shall teach the songs to our children. The songs shall not die, though many of us perish on this journey.

O God of paths in the sea, teach me more songs. I am your daughter of struggling faith, but I know how to dance. Lead me, and I will lead others in your dance of deliverance.

—*Jody Seymour*

WHAT HAS GOD BROUGHT YOU THROUGH THAT DESERVES YOUR HEART-FELT THANKS? WHAT HAS HE DONE THIS VERY DAY WITHOUT EVEN BEING ASKED, WITHOUT EVEN BEING NOTICED? WORSHIP HIM!

Miriam

OPPOSING GODLY LEADERSHIP

Selections from Numbers 12

It's late. Only a few couples are left around your kitchen table, sipping the last of your coffee— and carving up the pastor and the church for dessert. When they're gone, they'll leave behind a sinkful of dirty dishes. And wasted words that could have been prayers.

Miriam and Aaron criticized Moses because of the Cushite woman he married. . . . They said, "Does the LORD speak only through Moses? Does He not also speak through us?". . .

[The LORD] said: "Now listen to My words! . . . My servant Moses . . . he is faithful in all My household. I speak with him one on one openly, and not in riddles; he sees the form of the LORD. So why were you not afraid to speak against My servant Moses?"

So the LORD's anger burned against them, and He departed. As the cloud moved away from the tent, Miriam suddenly became leprous, like snow.

No pastor is perfect. No church leader is above all reproach. No husband or father can presume to always speak and act with the wisdom of God. Those in positions of godly authority over us—even the best of them—can't help but add some flesh into the mix of their decisions, some human undercurrents into their understanding of God's will. But God understands, and still admonishes folks like us to "Obey your leaders . . . so that they can do this with joy and not with grief, for that would be unprofitable for you" (Hebrews 13:17).

Look At It This Way

Miriam's dissatisfaction had probably been brewing for some time. If we could listen in to her conversations with herself, perhaps we would hear things such as: "There is something unfair about the organizational structure that is developing among us. Only men are being put in charge of things. Maybe that's the reason we're all stuck in the desert. . . . The women do not recognize and respect my role as prophetess. I really think Moses should require them to acknowledge my position. . . . I know that marrying a Cushite is not forbidden like marriage to a Canaanite, but it is beneath the spiritual position of our family."

We women have a way of stuffing our displeasure until it erupts. We also have a tendency to see life in its bits and pieces rather than as a part of the flow of redemption. When we look at the individual parts of our lives, some things appear unfair and unpleasant. When we take them out of the context of the big picture, we easily drift into the attitude that we deserve better, and the tumble down into the pit of pride begins.

—Susan Hunt

PRAY FOR YOUR LEADERS. PRAY THAT THEY'LL BE ABLE TO MAKE WISE DECISIONS, TO STAND AGAINST TEMPTATION, TO ENJOY UNITY IN THEIR HOMES. PRAYER WILL HELP KEEP YOU AT PEACE WITH THEM.

Daughters of Zelophehad
ADVOCATING CHANGE

Selections from Numbers 27

Ranting and raving about injustice with your like-minded sisters in the privacy of your own tent is one thing. It's quite another to take your case to the nation's leaders and right to the doorway of God. But sometimes you've got to stand and be heard.

The daughters of Zelophehad . . . stood before Moses, Eleazar the priest, the leaders, and the entire community, and said, "Our father died in the wilderness, but he himself was not among the faction, Korah's faction, that gathered together against the LORD. Instead, he died because of his own sin, and he had no sons.

"Why should the name of our father be taken away from his clan? Since he had no son, give us property among our father's brothers."

So Moses brought their case before the LORD, and the LORD said to Moses, "What Zelophehad's daughters say is right."

Is it okay for Christians to stand up for their rights? What about Christ's silent example? What about turning the other cheek? Let the nature of the offense determine whether you resist it or endure it. Are you being confronted with an issue that threatens your God-given rights to protect your family, express your convictions, or share your beliefs? Then stand and fight—for yourself and for others. But when the attack is personal, meant only to get a response, we should be willing to swallow hard and answer in gentleness.

Look At It This Way

Through love and conviction, any one average Joe or Joyce Citizen can make a difference. The system can still be made to work. When compassionate people realize this, they get involved—regardless of whether their involvement more closely resembles activism or ministry.

Opportunities to demonstrate love and justice are everywhere. God's people must act out their deeply held convictions in every area of their lives. That won't always be comfortable. Social action will stretch us beyond the familiar, the usual, the secure. But Jesus has called us to be risk-takers. By laying down our lives, we discover who we really are and what makes life worth living.

God asks none of us to change the world; that's beyond any individual's reach. He asks us only to work to improve our own corner of the world, however large or small that may be. It's far better to do something small than to sit, paralyzed by fear or apathy, and attempt nothing. Getting started takes just one small step: one phone call, one letter, one meeting, one prayer. Throw just one pebble into the pond. Who knows how far the ripples will reach?

—*Diane Hesselberg*

MANY OF OUR RIGHTS AS CHRISTIANS ARE UNDER FIRE TODAY, AND THERE'S MORE AT STAKE THAN OUR OWN HAPPINESS. CAN YOU THINK OF ANYTHING THAT YOU AND YOUR CHURCH CAN DO TO FIGHT BACK?

Rahab
UNEXPECTEDLY KIND

Selections from Joshua 2

Imagine the look on her face when two men from out of town arrived in her place of business. Imagine the surprise in their eyes when she agreed to stow them out of sight from the suspicious soldiers of Jericho's army. You never forget an unexpected kindness.

Joshua son of Nun secretly sent two men as spies, saying, "Go and scout the land, especially Jericho." So they left, and they came to the house of a woman, a prostitute named Rahab, and stayed there.... The king of Jericho sent to Rahab and said, "Bring out the men who came to you and entered your house, for they came to investigate the entire land." But the woman had taken the two men and hidden them....

She went up on the roof and said to them ... "Swear to me by the LORD that because I showed kindness to you, you will also show kindness to my family."

The spies found a brave, godly sort of kindness in a place they never expected—the home of a harlot. But what if *she* had been the one in genuine need—running for her life, a refugee in the camp of the Hebrews? Would this lady of the night have found the light of kindness in their eyes? Or would they have seen her for who she was, dropped their gaze from her disreputable appearance, and told her to look somewhere else for a handout? Should she have expected any more from God's people?

Look At It This Way

For Rahab, the mysterious process of conversion appears to have happened in the same way it does for each of us. According to his timing, when the moment was exactly right, the Lord planted faith deep within her hurting heart, and with absolute authority and irresistible loving-kindness, called her home.

We can only imagine what went through the spies' minds when they realized God was using this particular woman—a well-known Canaanite prostitute—to supply strong hope to Hebrew warriors. With stars glimmering overhead, the stalwart trio of unlikely heroes, gazing up at the heavens from a makeshift hideaway on a Jericho rooftop, cooperate with God in creating history.

A freshening breeze brings a cool night's respite to the sweltering city, accompanied by an unseen wind carrying truth to Rahab's mind, igniting her spirit with the healing heat of God's unfailing love. Lifted by the Creator's unchanging will from the shame and social confinement of her notorious harlotry, Rahab's humiliating legacy is exchanged without warning for a unique position of honor.

—Debra Evans

WE PASS BY SO MANY OPPORTUNITIES TO SHOW KINDNESS—UNEXPECTED KINDNESS—CHANCES THAT WOULD DO MORE FOR OUR WITNESS THAN ALL THE WORDS IN THE WORLD. BE EXPECTING SOME TODAY.

Deborah
TRUSTED LEADER

Selections from Judges 4

Deborah was one of those women who made you want to follow. Her strength of character and her wise, confident resolve won her a place of unrivaled leadership in Israel—and showed again that God can bring us success when our trust is in him.

[Deborah] summoned Barak . . . and said to him, "Has not the LORD, the God of Israel, commanded: 'Go, draw out your troops to Mount Tabor. Take with you 10,000 men from the Naphtalites and Zebulunites, and I will draw out Sisera, the commander of Jabin's forces, his chariots, and his army against you at the Wadi Kishon, and I will give him into your hands.' "

Barak replied, "If you will come with me, then I will go. But if you will not come with me, I will not go." She responded, "I will certainly go with you, but . . . you will reap no fame because the LORD will sell Sisera into a woman's hand."

Deborah was one of those women who did it all. She was a wife, a prophetess, a civic official, a judge, a worship leader. (Wow.) God seems to equip some people with an incredible load of talent and versatility. And those who make those gifts available for his use are able to accomplish amazing things with their twenty-four hours. Are you able to look at women like that and—without picking them apart or feeling the need to make excuses—thank God for what they do? And thank God for what he's given you to do?

Look At It This Way

Christian womanhood is at risk in our culture today. Women are hearing many voices with dazzling messages of self-actualization, self-fulfillment, self-promotion, and all the other self-approaches to life. We are in desperate need for women of faith who are willing to courageously stand against sin and stand for righteousness. But it is not enough for us to make this decision for ourselves and to carry the banner alone. We must motivate others to follow.

Christian women need to have a vision of women confidently and boldly serving the Lord God. We need to challenge them to lives of virtue and servanthood in order to glorify our glorious God. We cannot issue the challenge in a vacuum. We must be willing to make the investment, to give faithful instruction, to nurture, then to sound a clarion call to biblical womanhood.

Are there women who will step forward and bring their lives under the authority of God's Word regardless of the risks? Together we will celebrate a resurgence of virtuous living among the daughters of the King.

—*Susan Hunt*

YOU MAY FEEL THAT YOU DON'T HAVE A LOT OF INFLUENCE ON ANYBODY. BUT YOU DO. OFFER UP TO GOD YOUR TALENTS AND YOUR RELATIONSHIPS. AND BEGIN USING THEM TO EXTEND HIS KINGDOM.

Jael
COURAGEOUS CONVICTIONS

Careful now: What Jael did under the circumstances was big, bold, and brave. It's the kind of thing you do in wartime. But for those of us facing hostile enemies on the home front, the bravest thing we can do is fight back in ways that are prayerful and redemptive.

Sisera had fled on foot to the tent of Jael, wife of Heber the Kenite, because Jabin, king of Hazor, had a peace treaty with the family of Heber. . . . He instructed her, "Stand at the entrance to the tent. If a man should come and ask you, 'Is there a man here?' say, 'No.'"

Jael, Heber's wife, took a tent peg. . . . While Sisera was sleeping, totally exhausted . . . she hammered the peg into his temple and drove it on into the ground. And Sisera died. Look! At that moment Barak was pursuing Sisera. Jael went out to greet him and said, "Come! I will show you the man you are looking for."

Hers is one of the most gruesome pictures in the entire Bible—not exactly one of those stories that translates into a popular gift line, like Noah's Ark or Jacob's Ladder—because even though the land flowed with milk and honey, it also crawled with hostile nations who harassed God's people with unmerciful regularity. In the same way, we as Christians—though our lives flow with the milk and honey of forgiven sin—must deal with enemies in our camp, not to mention the trouble we cause our own selves through our unwise actions.

Look At It This Way

I have learned over the years that when one's mind is made up, this diminishes fear; knowing what must be done does away with fear.

When I sat down on the bus the day I was arrested, I had made up my mind about what it was that I had to do, what I felt was right to do. I did not think of being physically tired or fearful. After so many years of oppression and being a victim of the mistreatment that my people had suffered, not giving up my seat—and whatever I had to face after not giving it up—was not important. I did not feel any fear at sitting in the seat I was sitting in. All I felt was tired. Tired of being pushed around. Tired of seeing the bad treatment and disrespect of children, women, and men just because of the color of their skin. Tired of the Jim Crow laws. Tired of being oppressed. I was just plain tired.

God did away with all my fear. It was time for someone to stand up—or in my case, sit down. So I refused to move.

—Rosa Parks

IT TAKES A BRAVE WOMAN TO TAKE A STAND FOR HER CONVICTIONS —TO ENDURE CONFRONTA- TION AND SCORN FROM HER ACCUSERS (AND SOME- TIMES, MISUN- DERSTANDING FROM HER OWN FRIENDS). BE BOLD!

45

Manoah's Wife
TRUSTING GOD

Selections from Judges 13

Allowing her to become pregnant would have been answer enough. But sending an angel with the news—wow! She didn't know then all that would happen to her little boy Samson, but she had a strong suspicion God had something very big in mind.

His name was Manoah. His wife was barren and childless. The angel of the LORD appeared to the woman and said to her, "Look! . . . You will conceive and give birth to a son.". . . The woman went and told her husband. . . .

"We'll surely die," Manoah warned his wife, "because we've seen God."

"If the LORD desired to kill us," his wife assured him, "He wouldn't have accepted the burnt offering and the grain offering from our hands. And He wouldn't have shown us all these things. At this time, He wouldn't have spoken to us like this."

The two strikingly different reactions to God's presence by Manoah and his wife suggest that their marriage was like many we've seen—a woman walking in close fellowship with the Lord, her husband following at a distance. Manoah's wild-eyed panic that they had unwittingly done something to deserve death shows how thin the disguise of self-reliance really is. See his wife, though, grasping his hands to settle him down, forcing him to look into her face. *You don't know him like I do, honey. Trust me. He's a good God!*

Look At It This Way

Dear friend, I tell you the Lord is in your heart. Since the day of your conversion he has been dwelling there. During all that time, every moment might have been passed in the sunshine of his sweet presence and every step taken under his advice. But because you did not know it and did not look for him there, your life has been lonely and full of failure.

But now that I make you aware of this, how are you going to receive it? Are you glad to have him? Will you throw every door wide open to welcome him in? Will you joyfully and thankfully give up your life to him? Will you consult him about everything and let him decide each step and mark out every path? Will you invite him into your innermost chambers and share your most hidden life with him? Will you say "yes" to his longing for union with you? Will you, with a glad and eager surrender, hand yourself and all that concerns you over into his hands? If you will do this, your soul will begin to know something of the joy of union with Christ.

—Hannah Whitall Smith

HOW WE WILL REACT IN THE DIFFICULT TIMES, IN THE CHALLENGING SEASONS OF LIFE, DEPENDS ON HOW WELL WE'VE GOTTEN TO KNOW GOD WHEN IT'S NICE AND QUIET—IN THE ORDINARY EVERYDAY.

Delilah
FOR LOVE OF MONEY

Selections from *Judges 16*

There's not a single one of you who would do what Delilah did. Lower than low. But there is one little element of her story that disguises itself behind the more dramatic touches of ropes and looms. It's her main motivation. And sometimes it's ours. Money.

[Samson] fell in love with a woman in the Sorek Valley whose name was Delilah. The Philistine rulers approached her and told her, "Entice him, and find out the source of his great strength and how we can prevail against him. We will bind him so we can make him helpless. Each of us will give you 1,100 pieces of silver.". . .

Because she pestered him day after day with her words and begged him insistently, he became so impatient that he was ready to die. He told her all his heart. . . . So the Philistine rulers came up to her and brought the money in their hands. . . . She began to bring him under her control, and his strength left him.

*S*amson certainly turns out to be the idiot in this story. Tricked, tricked, then tricked some more by his smooth-talking seductress, he definitely wins the grand prize for stupidity. But even as he's led off to a Philistine workhouse, trapped by the cords of his own foolishness, don't you think Delilah is just as trapped by the endless entanglements of greed? Soon, all the money she's raked in from this little rendezvous will be turned into trinkets and temporary pleasures. Doesn't she know greed's got a bigger appetite than that?

Look At It This Way

Money has a good side and a bad side. Its good side is what it provides—daily needs for the family, support for the ministry, even a few enjoyable luxuries in life. Its bad side is what our love for money destroys—compassion, self-sacrifice, intense love for God.

The love of money, and what money can buy, creates havoc in many marriages. We each want what we want, and find ways to buy it. Then the bills and monthly payments stack up until we are at our limit. A genuine emergency occurs, and we're overwhelmed. Tensions rise as we each blame the other for spending too much or not earning enough. The good side of money becomes the bad side. What provided for our needs and pleasures has now turned into payments due and no way to pay. Resolving the conflict between husband and wife may bring temporary relief, but a lasting solution will not come until we submit our love for money to Christ, and bring our earning and spending into the kingdom of God. We must honor God with our finances before we can expect him to honor us with inner contentment.

—*Neil T. Anderson and Charles Mylander*

BE CAREFUL OF THE ROLE THAT MONEY PLAYS IN YOUR THINKING, IN YOUR DREAMING, IN YOUR CONSISTENT LIST OF WORRIES. MONEY ONLY HAS THE VALUE YOU GIVE IT. KEEP IT UNDER GOD'S CONTROL.

Orpah
THE COMFORT ZONE

Selections from Ruth 1

She had
already taken
a big leap,
marrying one
of the Hebrew
boys who had
come to Moab
to escape the
famine. But
now her man
was dead.
And with no
husband,
what would
her family
think if she
still found
something
worth going
to Judah for?

"Go back, my daughters!" Naomi insisted. "Why would you want to come with me? Do I have more sons in my womb, who would become your husbands? Return, my daughters! Leave! For I am far too old to have another husband. If I were to say that I am hopeful of having a husband this very night and of bearing sons, would you be willing to wait for them until they become men? Because of them, would you deny yourself the opportunity to marry another man? No, my daughters!"...

So they again cried out with weeping, and Orpah kissed her mother-in-law good-bye; but Ruth clung to her.

Orpah's decision basically boiled down to one dilemma. *Should I stay here at home where my needs will be met, or should I venture into the unknown to meet the needs of others?* Most of our decisions to choose either safety or surrender are determined by whether we're more concerned with keeping ourselves full or with pouring ourselves out so that others can be filled. There are times when staying behind is God's desire for us, but his call is always to serve—whether in the familiar or the foreign.

Look At It This Way

The junctures in our lives are very much like the crossroads that Ruth and Orpah faced. We might answer as Ruth did, saying, "Lord, I don't know what's ahead, but I'm ready to go, clinging only to You." But then again, we may be tempted to give Orpah's response: "Well, I feel bad about having to make this decision, but I'm going to stick it out in good old Moab."

Oh, Orpah was certainly sorry. She felt a pang of regret. The parting made her wistful and blue. But this type of sorrow produces very little change or fruitfulness. It's more like a vague depression that goes nowhere at all.

There is in every one of us an Orpah who will sigh, dab her eyes, and say, "Oh, I feel so bad. I feel so sorry. Following God to a new time and a new place sounds nice. But I think I'll just stay where I am. After all, it's what I know. It's where I'm comfortable." In such a way, Orpah slipped out the back door to Moab, her eyes on the old landmarks, her feet treading easily in the well-worn path.

—Jack Hayford

YOU MAY BE FACING A DECISION THAT'S FORCING YOU TO CHOOSE BETWEEN THE EASY AND THE ADVENTUROUS. HOW YOU DECIDE WILL TELL A LOT ABOUT HOW MUCH OF YOUR LIFE YOU'VE ENTRUSTED TO GOD.

Ruth

GOD'S WAY, HER WAY

Selections from Ruth 1

Two choices: Orpah chose the beaten path—her name reduced to a stumper question for Bible trivia fans. Ruth choose the path of unpredictability— no benefits, no retirement package, no promise of advancement. Now her name is in Jesus' royal line.

"Look," Naomi insisted, "your sister-in-law has gone back to her people and to her gods. Go back with your sister-in-law!"

"Don't force me to abandon you by turning back from following you," Ruth replied. "For wherever you may go, I will go; wherever you spend the night, I will spend the night; your people will be my people, and your God will be my God. . . . May the LORD bring on me whatever disaster He desires and even more if anything but death should separate you and me." When Naomi saw that Ruth insisted on going with her, she quit trying to persuade her. The two of them traveled on until they reached Bethlehem.

Ruth had a gentle spirit. She shines through the pages of Scripture as a woman of meekness and humility. So where did this spark of spunk come from? What was it about this one decision that brought her out of character, driving her to near defiance of the woman she loved more than any other? It's because Ruth had apparently defined her core beliefs. Years of living in this Hebrew family had stirred in her a passion for their customs, their way of life, their God. We all need something we'll go down fighting for.

Look At It This Way

Mahlon's widow patiently listens to Naomi's repetitious pleas. Over the years, she has grown to appreciate this stalwart matriarch's buoyant outlook. Ruth does not even attempt to argue with the wailing widow. She stands by, waiting for the right moment to vow her allegiance, impressed by Naomi's creative tactics.

But Ruth is not moved. Years of residing with this resilient Hebrew woman has profoundly influenced Ruth, providing her with a new identity that cannot be instantly discarded at will along an arid road east of town.

Return to Chemosh? The worthless idol Naomi hates? To Moab, where regularly scheduled human sacrifices fail to satiate the demon's hunger? Back to the place where Mahlon is buried and family ties remain permanently changed by the strain of an interfaith alliance? Away from the lasting comfort of a mother who speaks of the living God with steadfast loyalty and tender conviction? Never.

The sorrowful scene shifts. Naomi notices that Ruth's wet face has a radiant glow. For once in her life, Elimelech's widow is at a loss for words.

—*Debra Evans*

TURNING BACK IS ALWAYS AN OPTION, LOSING SIGHT OF OUR CALLING AND MISSING THE OPPORTUNITIES THAT AWAIT US JUST BEYOND THE UNKNOWN. OR WE CAN TAKE GOD'S HAND AND WALK . . . HIS WAY.

Ruth
HEARTFELT SINCERITY

Ruth was a vulnerable, impoverished young widow in a field full of burly work-men, with good reason to be intimidated by the wealth and influence of their big boss, Boaz. But no mat-ter whom she encountered, whether great or small, she was always just herself.

[Ruth] fell on her face, bowed to the ground, and asked [Boaz], "Why are you so gracious to me that you pay so much attention to me, a foreign woman?"

Boaz answered her, "Everything you've done for your mother-in-law since your husband's death has been fully reported to me. You left your father and your mother and the land where you were born. You came to a people with whom you had no experience. May the LORD reward what you've done. May you receive your wages in full from the LORD God of Israel, under whose wings you have come for refuge."

Ruth's story seems like one long string of coincidences. She just happened to be going out to glean one day, and just happened to find herself on Boaz's land, who just happened to have heard of Ruth's troubles and of her kindness to Naomi—and who just happened to be a rich relative with the power to change Ruth's whole lot in life. If you were to ask her why she chose Boaz's grain field, she'd just say that she liked the look of it. But something tells you that God was in the coincidence.

Look At It This Way

Qualities such as availability, simplicity, and unaffectedness are difficult to come by. Fear makes us pretend, masquerade, play our people games, or flirt with insincerity. But God seeks honest hearts. He longs to deliver us from anything less than genuine or anything flavored by the cynical. This prideful attitude hamstrings our ability to move into the fresh and the new . . . and grieves the Spirit of God.

Who says you know what's next for your life? Who says God can't use you in a dramatic, wholly unexpected way? Who says he can't lead you into a season of life and ministry beyond anything you've ever experienced—or even dreamed? Just who is the limiting factor here? Is it God? Or are we capable of closing our hearts to what he wants to do in and through our lives? Ruth is as simple and honest as a field lily, as openhearted as a child. It is a spiritual beauty we can all learn from. No wonder Boaz lost his heart in the barley field that spring morning! Ruth had prepared herself to step out in faith and see what this God of Israel had to offer.

—Jack Hayford

BEING YOURSELF IS STILL THE BEST WAY TO KEEP YOUR EMOTIONS IN BALANCE, YOUR PERSPECTIVE INTACT, YOUR RELATIONSHIPS HONEST—AND TO KEEP THE KEYS TO YOUR HEART IN THE HANDS OF GOD.

Ruth

SHARING HER PLENTY

Selections from Ruth 2

Ruth knew that whatever barley she ate herself was that much more she had to go out and glean tomorrow. Whatever she gave away meant even more back-breaking work and long hours in the hot sun. But givers choose to forget little things like that.

When it was time to eat, Boaz invited [Ruth], "Come over here and eat some of our bread. . . ." She sat beside the harvesters, and he offered her some roasted grain. . . .

When Ruth got up to return to gleaning, Boaz ordered his young male servants, "Let her even glean among the sheaves, but never humiliate her.". . . She gleaned in his field until evening. When she threshed out what she had gleaned, she had about half a bushel of barley. She picked it up and went into town. Her mother-in-law saw how much she had gleaned, and then Ruth brought out and gave what remained from her meal to Naomi.

Most of the time, we equate giving only with money and limit the targets of our giving to the homeless, hungry, and impoverished. But to really give as we should, we should follow Ruth's example, realizing that everything we possess is a potential gift to someone—food, clothing, time, books, even tulip bulbs. And this too: If we can learn to develop a giving heart toward those in our own homes and families, we'll be much more free to give ungrudgingly—and at the Spirit's prompting—to those in the most desperate need.

Look At It This Way

Learning to be a giver is probably the most important habit you can learn in your quest to become financially responsible. Being a generous person, one whose giving is so habitual it is almost automatic, will bring balance not only to your finances but also to your life.

Do you have a secret little problem with greed? Give! Is it tough to make the money last as long as the month? Give! Are you fearful of the future—afraid you will run out of resources, financial or otherwise? Give! Do you somehow feel your success and personal identity are tied to the balance in your checkbook? Give! When you are the neediest is when you should give the most.

I don't know of anything that will take your eyes off your own situation faster than giving to others. If you want your life to have purpose, your finances to come into balance, and your faith increased, become a giver! Part of everything we have is ours to give away. If you really believe that, your attitudes will begin to reflect it and your life will be greatly enriched.

—*Mary Hunt*

MOST OF US HAVE SO MUCH MORE THAN WE NEED— EVEN THINGS WE NO LONGER WANT THAT COULD BE OF USE TO SOMEONE ELSE. TAKE INVENTORY OF YOUR PLENTY, AND GIVE A LITTLE MORE THAN YOU CAN.

Ruth
WISELY SEEKING A HUSBAND

Knowing Ruth's fondness for Naomi, we can only assume that her marriage to Naomi's son had been a happy one. So let's learn from someone who had walked the aisle once and was willing to do it again. There's no man like the right man.

When Boaz had eaten and drunk and was enjoying life, he went in to lie down at the end of the pile of grain. Then [Ruth] went in secretly, uncovered his legs, and lay down. At midnight, the man awoke with a start and turned over. He was shocked to find a woman lying at his feet.

"Who are you?" he demanded.

"I am Ruth, your humble servant," she replied. . . .

"May the LORD bless you, my daughter," he replied. "You have made your latest act of faithful love better than your first one by not going after the young men, whether poor or rich."

*I*f you still have children at home who are not yet marrying age, begin consistently praying for their wisdom in choosing a godly wife or husband when the time comes. And don't just pray about it by yourself during your drive-time or private devotions, but pray along with them. That's not forcing their hand toward marriage but helping them to see how serious an impact this one choice will have on their life . . . and how much God must love them to be watching out for them so far in advance.

Look At It This Way

As I stand on this side of matrimony with no potential mate in sight, I still have so many questions. Will I know when I'm walking through the story for the first time? Will I recognize the event that will begin the chapters of my love story with my mate? Will time stand still for one moment to tell me that this person—this one person, out of all the billions bustling on the planet—is the one?

Some questions are probably best left unasked. I know I should push them aside and wait for life to unfold its mysteries. Someday when I'm older and wiser, I'll probably tell some young fool the same things I get so tired of hearing from others. I'll tell him to bide his time, "for it's sure to work out in the end." And, of course, "you can't rush these things."

How will you respond when one day you look back on your love story? Will it bring tears of joy or tears of remorse? Will it remind you of God's goodness or your lack of faith in his goodness? Will it be a story of purity, faith, and selfless love? Or will it be a story of impatience, selfishness, and compromise? It's your choice.

—*Joshua Harris*

GOD CAN TRANSFORM ANY MARRIAGE AT ANY STAGE OF THE TRIP—AND MAKE IT BETTER THAN IT WAS WHEN IT STARTED—WHEN WE WISELY SEEK TO SERVE HIM, AND IN TURN TO SERVE EACH OTHER.

Naomi
EMBITTERED

Selections from Ruth 1

---

*There are
some things
that aren't
supposed to
happen. Like
outliving your
two sons. Or
like watching
all your plans
for a better
life disappear
into the dust
of your hus-
band's grave.
It's hard to
count your
blessings when
you're count-
ing alone.*

Naomi's husband Elimelech died, leaving her alone with her two sons. . . . She rose with her daughters-in-law and turned her back on Moabite territory, having heard in Moab that the LORD had visited His people to give them food. . . . As they entered Bethlehem, the entire town went wild over them, and the local women wondered, "Is this Naomi?"

"Don't call me Naomi!" she told them. "Call me Mara—because the Almighty has made me very bitter. I left here with a full family, but the LORD has brought me back empty. Why do you call me 'Naomi' when the LORD has testified against me?"

*M*oab literally means *ease*, and Bethlehem means *house of bread*. Naomi and her family, scared away by famine, left the land of God—the "house of bread"—to go to the land of ease. They were hoping to find some relief from their troubles, unaware how costly life in Moab would be. Yet widowed, homesick, and alone, Naomi looked past their poor choices and saw a God who deserved all the blame. How easy it is to forget God's face in the pleasant times, only to see his hand everywhere in the bad.

Look At It This Way

You could be a devoted young mother who must watch her two-year-old child die slowly of cancer while you overhear other parents worry about their children's scratched knees and bruised elbows. You could be a 39-year-old single woman who has served God faithfully for decades and has always longed to be married, only to watch your spiritually shallow 25-year-old friend wed a wonderful godly man.

Life isn't fair. Inequities hit us from all sides, prompting those wretched "I'm a victim" feelings. But Scripture presents us with a view of life from the eternal perspective. This perspective separates what is transitory from what is lasting. What is transitory, such as injustice and injury, will not endure; what is lasting, such as the eternal weight of glory accrued from that pain, will remain forever.

What could possibly outweigh the pain of permanent paralysis, the pain of a life of singleness, the loss of a child from cancer? The greater weight of eternal glory. One day the scales of justice will not only balance, but they will be weighted heavily—almost beyond comprehension—to our good and God's glory.

—Joni Eareckson Tada

BITTERNESS IS BORN WHEN WE HOLD ON TOO TIGHTLY TO THE THINGS—EVEN THE PEOPLE—IN OUR LIVES. TREASURE EVERY MOMENT AS A PRECIOUS GIFT FROM GOD, BUT NEVER CLAIM IT AS A RIGHT.

Naomi
HANGING IN THERE

Never in her wildest dreams had Naomi seen herself holding a grandson. But look at her now— bouncing him on her knee, tickling him under his chin to see that little dimple one more time. Is this the same Naomi who once had nothing left to live for?

Boaz took Ruth, and she became his wife. . . . The LORD caused her to conceive, and she gave birth to a son. The women said to Naomi, "Blessed be the LORD, who has not withheld a kinsman-redeemer from you today. May the boy's name be famous in Israel. He will restore your life for you, providing for you in your old age. For your daughter-in-law, who loves you and who is better to you than seven sons, has given birth to him."

Naomi took the child, laid him in her lap, and became his constant attendant. The neighbor women gave him a name, saying, "A son has been born to Naomi."

Driven by famine and the hungry looks on her boys' faces, Naomi had gone along with her husband's decision to head for greener pastures in Moab. But who cares about food when your husband dies, then your two sons both die, and you're left all alone except for two widowed daughters-in-law—whom you're convinced are only hanging around because they feel sorry for you? She never thought she'd smile again, or look up into the sunshine and be glad she was alive. But hang in there, Naomi. God's not through with you yet.

Look At It This Way

Outside Monrovia, Liberia, is a little village named Harbell built on the site of a former Firestone rubber plantation. In the village a small church and school have been established to serve the displaced persons who live there. The pastor of the church is named Gabriel, and the headmaster of the church-run school is named Emmanuel. The school serves six hundred children and has no books, pencils, paper, or blackboard. When the pastor was asked if he was discouraged, he looked amazed and said, "We are Christians. We may be helpless, but we are not hopeless!"

Are you a Christian? If you are, how can you be hopeless? Are you so depressed by the greatness of your problems that you have given up all hope? Instead of giving up, would you patiently endure? Would you focus on Christ until you are so preoccupied with him alone that you fall prostrate before him?

And if you never feel the hand of God on your life, if you never hear the voice of God calling you into service, it will be enough to lie at his feet and gaze upon the vision of his glory!

—*Anne Graham Lotz*

ARE YOU IN A DARK, DESPONDENT TIME? BELIEVE THIS TODAY: "GOD IS FAITHFUL" IS MORE THAN A CONSOLATION PRIZE. HE CAN SEE YOU THROUGH THE STORM. AND MAKE YOU LIVE TO TELL ABOUT IT.

 Hannah
CLINGING TO A DREAM

Selections from 1 Samuel 1

Sometimes we must experience the hurts of life without benefit of sympathetic counselors or understanding friends. Like Hannah, we must sometimes fight our struggle alone. Yet not really alone, for God is always a prayer away.

With a grieved soul Hannah prayed to the LORD and wept bitterly. Making a vow she pleaded, "O LORD of Hosts, if You will take notice of Your handmaid's affliction and remember me and not forget me and give Your handmaid a son, then I will give him to the LORD all the days of his life.". . . Although her lips were moving, her voice couldn't be heard, so Eli concluded that she was drunk. . . . "Oh no, my lord," Hannah replied. . . . "I've been pouring out my soul before the LORD.". . .

Eli responded, "Go in peace and may the God of Israel grant the petition that you've requested from Him."

*N*ever dream without prayer. When we talk to others about the dreams in our lives, we often get blind stares of disinterested discouragement—roadblocks, rejection. But when we take our dreams to God, we begin an adventurous journey of faith. It may mean being broken along the way, but only to let our dream escape. It may mean going through seasons of searching, but only to determine how much of our dream is selfish—and to prove how badly we really want God's way. Prayer keeps holy dreams alive.

Look At It This Way

Hannah was tested. Her rival-as-wife, Peninnah, taunted her relentlessly. Hannah was further upset each time she went to the temple at Shiloh. There, in the midst of families going to offer their worship and their sacrifices, she felt all alone without a child.

When his two wives were at each other's throats, Elkanah would try to smooth things over by asking, "Don't I mean more to you than ten sons?" What she needed and longed to hear from him was that she meant more *to him* than ten sons. God was using everyone in this woman's life to test her.

We are tested so our character will match our dreams. Christian character is a work in progress for us as believers. When God gives us a dream, we may need a lot of work on and in our lives to enable us to handle the dream. Our sufficiency and strength should always be in God—and God alone. As with Hannah, it usually is a pretty good clue that the test or the dream is from God when things don't work out easily. The greater the dream, the greater the testing.

—*Jim Henry*

DO YOU HAVE A DREAM THAT FEELS LIKE IT'S DYING IN YOUR LIFE? DON'T GIVE UP. TAKE IT TO GOD IN PRAYER TODAY. AND TRUST HIM TO DO MORE WITH YOUR DREAM THAN YOU COULD EVER DO YOURSELF.

Hannah
RELEASING HER CHILD

Selections from 1 Samuel 1

If you've ever dared one more hug before watching your son drive off in a car crammed to the rooftop with everything he owns, you've been in Hannah's world. You've fought back her tears, you've tried not to look into his bedroom, you've let go.

When [Hannah] had weaned him, she took him, along with a three-year-old bull, two and one-half gallons of flour, and a jar of wine, with her up to Shiloh. Even though the boy was young, she took him to the LORD's house at Shiloh. Then they slaughtered the bull and took the boy to Eli.

She said . . . "I'm the woman who was standing here beside you praying to the LORD. It was for this boy I prayed, and since the LORD granted me what I requested from Him, I now grant the boy to the LORD. For as long as he lives, he is granted to the LORD." Then he worshiped the LORD there.

How hard it must have been for Hannah to keep her promise—her prayerful plea that, if God would give her a son, she would return him for a life of full-time service to his Lord. On warm sunny days, when Samuel's playful laughter would catch her ear, she'd look up from her work and wish she could bottle her feelings . . . and almost wish she could rescind that costly vow. But in her heart, she knew what she had to do. Doing the right thing when your feelings scream not to—that's Hannah's legacy.

Look At It This Way

Our Creator, who divided the year into seasons and the days into mornings and nights, also divided people into families. He created this gift of a structure to offer stability and loving security in the midst of an unstable and insecure world. He intended families to be the safe haven where children are born and raised, a place where the tender shoots are nurtured until their roots grow strong and deep.

But that nurturing process has a purpose and time frame. We raise our children to leave us. We take care of them while we're teaching them to take care of themselves. We transfer freedom and responsibility from our own shoulders to theirs in a slow and orderly process as they grow up. When that task nears completion, we let go, and they go off on their own. That's part of God's plan for families in the changing seasons of life.

At first, I felt angry about the unfairness of it all. I asked God, "Why did You give us the gift of family—and then take it away?" Now I know He does not take family away. He merely changes its shape.

—Carol Kuykendall

ARE YOU DOING ALL YOU CAN TO PREPARE YOUR CHILDREN FOR LIFE? ARE YOU MODELING FOR THEM THE ATTITUDES AND BEHAVIORS OF A GODLY WOMAN? ARE YOU READY TO GO TO A NEW LEVEL OF TRUST IN GOD?

Abigail
PERSISTENT PEACEMAKER

Selections from 1 Samuel 25

Abigail was able to see the far-reaching implications of her husband's actions long before he could. She knew that his gruff old growlings were about to cost him more than he could pay. Heaven knew he deserved it. But after all, he was her husband.

When Abigail saw David, she quickly got off the donkey and fell on her face in David's presence, bowing to the ground.... "My lord should pay no attention to this scoundrel Nabal, for he lives up to his name: Nabal is his name, and folly is with him.". . .

Then David said to Abigail, "Blessed is the LORD God of Israel, who sent you to meet me today! Blessed is your discernment, and blessed are you. Today you kept me from participating in bloodshed and avenging myself through my own hand. . . . Go home in peace. See, I have heard what you said and have granted your request."

*Y*ou might call Abigail's brand of peacemaking more like intercession—like Abraham's standing in the gap between Sodom and certain destruction, pleading with God to make an exemption for his poor nephew, Lot. But perhaps all peacemaking must begin in a similar spot—in prayer to God, interceding for another, asking blessing for the one who has cursed us, and opening our own hearts for godly examination. When peacemaking is born and raised in prayer, we can be at peace with the situation no matter how it turns out.

Look At It This Way

There are those who question the wisdom of Abigail's speedy actions. They wonder whether she preempted God by intruding where she did not belong. But the king's affirmation of her hazardous service to the God of Israel says something else. And although it is impossible to know her innermost thoughts and true motives, Abigail appears to have properly feared God and Israel's appointed king more than she feared her cantankerous husband. Would the biblical record portray her as wise or show her in a favorable light if this had not been the case? Surely, the meeting with David presents Abigail as a remarkable example of humility, service, and obedience.

For a woman of faith who finds herself in a relationship with a man in rebellion against God, peacemaking is sometimes thought to mean avoiding confrontations, burying the truth, and smiling through the pain. But through Abigail's valiant witness, we see faithfulness and obedience to the king rewarded. Clearly, staying silent is not always what God directs a woman to do.

—Debra Evans

WHEN YOU CONSIDER GOD'S DESIRE FOR YOU TO MAKE PEACE, CAN YOU SEE NAMES AND FACES IN YOUR MIND—PEOPLE WHO ARE IN NEED OF YOUR COMPASSIONATE INTERVENTION OR YOUR UNCONDITIONAL FORGIVENESS?

Michal
CRITICIZING OTHERS' WORSHIP

Selections from 2 Samuel 6

Perched high in a palace window, far above the nuisance of the noisy crowd, Michal could hardly believe what she was seeing—the king dancing like a crazy man, right out in front of God and everybody. She'll learn that worship is no spectator sport.

As the ark of the LORD was entering the City of David, Saul's daughter Michal looked out the window and saw King David leaping and dancing before the LORD, and she despised him in her heart. . . . "How the king of Israel honored himself today!" she said. "He revealed himself today in the sight of his servants' maids just like one of the worthless people would reveal himself!"

David replied to Michal . . . "I'll continue to celebrate before the LORD, and I'll demean myself more than this and consider myself lowly. As for the maids of whom you spoke, by them I'll be honored."

God has given each of us a certain demeanor, a specific temperament. And it reflects itself in the way we worship. Some people like it loud and rowdy—and don't understand why others can't get in the Spirit. Some respond to God in quiet, reflective reverence, contemplating His wonder and goodness with their heads bowed, their hands folded—bewildered by all the noise and activity. So let's relax. And be ourselves. And let God enjoy the symphony we create when we worship Him just the way He made us to.

Look At It This Way

If you've ever held back from expressing your faith in God for fear that someone might criticize . . . If you've ever looked with envy at exuberant Christians and wondered why they had what you didn't . . . If you've ever sat in a worship service and felt somehow cheated because you didn't feel free to express the exaltation you saw those around you expressing . . . If you haven't dared to dance with God because of the eyebrows you might raise . . . welcome to the Michalepsy ward.

There's never been a short supply of uptight critics to scold Christians who sang too loud, raised their hands too high, or amened too often. Their smirks and quips are designed to keep the worship of God from becoming too brazen, too raucous, too anything. And they are with us today. Michal was just the first in a long line of church police who see it as their mission in life to insure that praising—if done at all—is done with refinement and propriety.

Michal's end should convince us that criticizing the praise of others is not a dance that God will join us in.

—Jeff Walling

LET'S LET PEOPLE WORRY MORE ABOUT PLEASING GOD THAN US WITH THEIR PRAISE. THE WORSHIP VEHICLES WE DRIVE ARE NOT NEARLY AS IMPORTANT AS THE PLACES THEY TAKE US.

Tamar

REELING FROM ABUSE

Selections from 2 Samuel 13

Few things are more tragic in a person's life than the violation of their innocence. Through the perpetuated misery of another's torment, one steals from another what can never be returned. It can happen even in the best of families.

> Tamar took the cakes she had made and went to her brother Amnon's bedroom. When she approached him so he could eat, he grabbed her and said to her, "Come lie with me, my sister!"
>
> "Don't, my brother!" she replied. "Don't humiliate me! . . . Don't commit this outrage! As for me, where could I go with my disgrace?". . . But he refused to listen to her, and since he was stronger than she, he overpowered her and lay with her. . . .
>
> Tamar put ashes on her head and tore the long-sleeved robe she was wearing. She put her hand on her head and left, weeping as she went.

A closer look at the biblical record reveals how something like this could happen even in a family like King David's. Nathan the prophet had warned him: "The sword will never depart from your house because you despised Me and took the wife of Uriah the Hittite to be your own wife" (2 Samuel 12:10). Our actions as parents are nothing more than seeds that will bear either ripe or rotten fruit in the lives of our children. And innocent kids like Tamar can get hurt badly in the process. We owe them better.

Look At It This Way

Feelings of revenge, bitterness, and unforgiveness ultimately hurt us more than they hurt the other person. Often we feel, "I'm never going to let go of my anger. I'll get even by not forgiving." Meanwhile, the other person is pursuing his own life and is not affected by our unforgiveness.

When we refuse to forgive a person, we actually become more bonded to him. The one we want distance from becomes the focal point of our thought life and sometimes of our behavior. This in turn keeps the anger and bitterness alive and growing. Forgiveness means that we acknowledge that the deed was indeed horrible, sinful, evil, dastardly, hurtful. There would be no need for forgiveness or repentance if there had been no violation.

Forgiveness breaks the power of the enemy in our lives. Forgiveness and right action begin the process of restoration and conformity to God's image. As this occurs, blessings begin to flow. We have more energy to think, to plan, to love and enjoy life rather than focusing obsessively on the misdeeds of others. The enemy no longer has permission to rob us of our joy.

—Normajean Hinders

YOU MAY NEVER TOTALLY ERASE THE TENDERNESS OF YOUR OWN SCARS, BUT YOU CAN MAKE SURE THE PAIN ENDS WITH YOU. TRUST GOD FOR THE POWER TO BREAK THE CYCLE OF ABUSE IN YOUR FAMILY.

Rizpah
DEATH IN THE FAMILY

Selections from 2 Samuel 21

A mother's love can make you do things you'd never expect—like sleep sitting straight up with a sick child or yell at the umpire who called your son out at third base. But some must do the truly unthinkable—stand at a graveside and promise to somehow go on.

David asked the Gibeonites, "What should I do for you? How can I make restitution so you will bless the inheritance of the LORD?"... They replied to the king, "Let seven of [Saul's] male descendants be handed over to us so we may hang them before the LORD at Gibeah of Saul—the chosen of the LORD."...

They were executed in the first days of the harvest.... Rizpah, Aiah's daughter, took sackcloth and spread it out for herself on the rock from the beginning of the harvest until the rain poured down from heaven onto the bodies. She didn't let the birds of the sky settle on them by day or the wild animals by night.

A teenager opens fire in a crowded school, and young lives end on the playground of innocence. A rare disease causes a couple's child to feel more at home in a hospital than in his own bedroom, until the day he closes his eyes—and goes home forever. The mother who must bury her own son or daughter comes the closest to understanding the love of God, the anguish of his heart, the cost of her salvation. And the woman who holds on through the storm realizes just how far God's comfort can travel.

Look At It This Way

We live in a world gone wrong, one that was created perfect, but now suffers the ravages of sin: death, violated relationships, children born with disabilities and deformities, disease, man's inhumanity to man, moral failures, tragedies of major proportions, chaos. It is, indeed, a broken world.

But it is one thing to shake our heads at the mess the world is in; it is quite another to confront the reality of it in our own lives. One layer away, it is sad. But when it hits us, it is ominous.

When we stand in the middle of a life-storm, it seems as if the storm has become our way of life. We cannot see a way out. We are unable to chart a course back to smoother waters. We feel defeated—and broken. Will that brokenness produce a cynicism that will keep us forever in the mire of "if-only" thinking? Or will we yield up that brokenness to the resources of One who calms the winds and the waves, heals the brokenhearted, and forgives the most grievous of sins? The choice is ours.

—*Verdell Davis*

HAVE YOU SHIED AWAY FROM THOSE WHO ARE SUFFERING, AFRAID YOU'LL SAY THE WRONG THING—OR THAT YOU'LL HAVE NOTHING TO SAY AT ALL? TRUST THOSE WHO'VE BEEN THERE. YOUR PRESENCE SPEAKS VOLUMES.

Bathsheba
INTERCEDING

You know her better, of course, for her well-known rendezvous with a wayward King David. But this time she comes to his bedside on business, not pleasure—pleading her case for Solomon's kingship, begging David to keep a lifelong promise.

"My lord, you swore to your maidservant by the LORD your God, 'Your son Solomon is to become king after me, and he is the one who is to sit on my throne.' And now, look! Adonijah has become king! . . . My lord king, the eyes of all Israel are on you to report back to them: Who will sit upon the throne of my lord the king after him? Otherwise, when my lord the king rests with his forefathers, I and my son Solomon will be regarded as criminals.". . .

The king swore an oath and said . . . "Your son Solomon is to become king after me, and he is the one who is to sit on my throne in my place."

*B*athsheba made her request to David, but her example reveals some important elements in the way we make our requests known to God. By going right into David's room, she reminds us that we have direct access to God's presence through our mediator, Jesus Christ, who "always lives to intercede" for us (Hebrews 7:25). And by basing her requests on David's spoken promise, she points out the spiritual fact that when we ask God for anything according to his Word, we are asking according to his will.

Look At It This Way

God has designed His kingdom so that Christians with kindred spirits join together. Often, God will graciously bring another believer alongside you who will undergird you in the work and the concerns God has placed on your heart. The Bible says that when two or more Christians meet and reverently discuss matters concerning the Lord, God is pleased to listen to them and to respond to their concerns.

If you are carrying concerns about your family or your church or your friends, ask God to bring likeminded believers around you to share the burden with you in conversation and in prayer. Don't attempt to bear your load of cares on your own. You may pray about them, but you will miss the blessing of uniting together with a group of believers who join together to intercede for one another and to enjoy God's presence.

Everything God has woven into the fabric of his kingdom promotes interdependence, not individualism. As you face your concerns, deliberately seek out other believers with whom you can stand and share your load.

—Henry Blackaby

OUR PRAYERS TEND TO BE MOSTLY ABOUT US. ARE YOU COMMITTING ENOUGH OF YOUR TIME TO FELLOWSHIP WITH GOD THAT YOU CAN GET BEYOND YOUR OWN NEEDS AND LIFT UP THE NEEDS OF OTHERS?

Compassionate Mother
PUTTING HER CHILD FIRST

Selections from 1 Kings 3

Solomon generally gets most of the glory here for showcasing his wisdom with such clarity and authority. But the real hero is an unnamed woman who represents millions of moms— women who know they'd do the exact same thing she did.

Two women who were prostitutes came to the king. . . . One woman said . . . "This woman's son died during the night when she lay on him. Then she got up in the middle of the night and took my son from my side.". . . But the other woman said, "No! My son is the living one, and your son is the dead one.". . .

The king said, "Cut the living boy in two and give half to the one and half to the other." The woman whose son was the living one spoke to the king . . . "Please, my lord, have them give her the living baby," she said, "but by no means have him killed!"

The king responded . . . "She is his mother."

The mother in this classic story had only a few days to complete a journey that most of us get twenty years to grow into—releasing our children from our own care into the waiting hands of life. Her sacrificial decision reminds us that we should never enter a day without realizing that our children are not our own— whether they're six months, six years, or sixteen. We are preparing them to outlive us, to become the people God created them to be, to discover their true source of worth in the trustworthy arms of God.

Look At It This Way

You stand in the doorway gazing wistfully at your daughter who is nearing sleep. Kneeling beside her bed, you bury your face in her hair and whisper your love into its fragrant softness. Half awake, she senses your presence and puts her arms around your neck, pulling your head hard against the side of her face. The embrace only lasts for a moment, then sleep reclaims her, and her arms grow limp. Carefully, you tuck the covers around her before planting a soft kiss on her forehead.

In the doorway, you glance back a final time. How desperately you wish that she could know the depth of your love. You cannot tell her, for there are no words to express what you feel. Even if there were, and if she could somehow comprehend their meaning, the totality of your love would still escape her. Softly you whisper, "Good night, my little one."

Tiptoeing down the hall, you comfort yourself with the knowledge that someday she will understand how you feel—someday when she becomes a mother and has a child of her own.

—*Richard Exley*

MOTHERS, TAKE A MOMENT TO THANK GOD AGAIN FOR THE GIFT OF YOUR CHILDREN. AND CHILDREN, THANK GOD AGAIN FOR THE GIFT OF YOUR MOTHER. WE NEED TO SAY THANKS A WHOLE LOT MORE.

Queen of Sheba
SEEKING WISDOM

Selections from 1 Kings 10

She didn't just set off in her royal coach for nothing or gift wrap gold bars for just anyone. But even a lady of pomp and power realizes that those things aren't enough. Those who go out of their way to seek wisdom find something of lasting value.

The queen of Sheba, having heard of Solomon's fame in connection with the name of the LORD, came to test him with difficult questions. . . . So Solomon answered all her questions. . . .

She said to the king, "The report I heard in my own country about your words and about your wisdom is true. But I didn't believe the reports until I came and saw with my own eyes. Indeed, I was not even told half! You far exceed in wisdom and prosperity the report I heard. . . . May the LORD your God be praised! He delighted in you and put you on the throne of Israel because of the LORD's eternal love for Israel."

$\mathcal{K}$nowledge can be learned, but wisdom must be earned. Wisdom is knowledge . . . lived. And that's why our wisdom, at whatever stage of life we find ourselves, is limited to our own experience until we surround ourselves with people who have walked this road before—godly men and women who have seen God's truth in action, precious grandparents who understand the cost of discipleship, and the writers of the ages whose words make the climb across time to teach a new generation. Seek wisdom. It's out there.

Look At It This Way

I think we Christians have become lazy. We would rather read a book about how someone else became closer to God than spend time alone with him ourselves. We would rather listen to someone else's interpretation of the Word of God than read it for ourselves. And yet we alone are accountable for what we believe. We can't stand before God on the day of judgment and explain that our incredible ignorance is our pastor's fault. It is our responsibility to access God's Word for ourselves.

There is nothing more important than understanding God's truth and being changed by it, so why are we so casual about accepting the popular theology of the moment without checking it out for ourselves? God has given us a mind so that we can learn and grow. As his people, we have a great responsibility and wonderful privilege of growing in our understanding of him. If marriages could be saved and children's lives made richer by study and understanding and change, think of the impact on the church if we as individual Christians befriended the spiritual discipline of study!

—*Sheila Walsh*

"WHATEVER ELSE YOU GET, GET UNDERSTANDING" (PROVERBS 4:7). THOUGH IT COSTS TIME, A LITTLE SLEEP, YOUR TV NIGHT, OR A SUMMER NOVEL, YOU'VE GOT TO DECIDE WHOSE WISDOM YOU WANT.

Widow of Zarephath
TRUSTING GOD'S PROVISION

Selections from 1 Kings 17

You don't have to be an impoverished widow to find yourself concerned about your future. Even a Bible hero like Elijah could come up against the hard edge of hunger. But watch how God can meet both of their needs in one fluid motion.

[Elijah] called to her and said, "Please bring me a piece of bread in your hand." But she said . . . "I don't even have a biscuit, only a handful of flour in the jar and a bit of oil in the jug. And here I am, gathering a couple of sticks in order to go prepare it for myself and my son so we may eat it and die."

Then Elijah said to her, "Don't be afraid; go and do as you have said. Only make me a small loaf from it and bring it out to me.". . . So she proceeded to do according to the word of Elijah. She and he and her household ate for many days. The flour jar didn't become empty, and the oil jug didn't run out.

Sorry, I can't help you. You can bet that's the first thought that ran through this widow's mind after Elijah asked her for a drink . . . *oh, and a little something to eat too, if you don't mind.* It's also our customary response to those who ask for our help—especially when (like the widow) we're preoccupied with our own problems. But what would happen if we'd make the same brave decision she did to meet someone else's hunger first? Sure, she had a nice promise to go on. But come to think of it, so do we.

Look At It This Way

I stared at the stack of bills piled high on my kitchen table just begging to be paid. The happy voices of my daughter and her two visiting cousins pushed into my mind. I worried their laughter might wake little Amy, who had finally fallen asleep after fussing with an ear infection all morning. They were digging up the dirt, throwing it into the air, feeling the goodness of the earth and sun and smiling at one another.

I cringed as I considered the contrast between their free spirits and my fearful, worried mind. Moments before, I had asked God for assurances about our income for the entire year. I wanted good health for my family now and forever more. Fairy tale wishes of a life without problems clouded my communication with God. I call them "worry prayers." They're not really productive—just a righteous way to worry.

I called the kids in for lunch. And I thought, Jesus has enough to take care of all my needs, but he does it only as I choose moment by moment to trust him. For this moment, all I need is to sit down and listen.

—*Marsha Crockett*

IT DOESN'T REQUIRE MUCH TRUST WHEN YOUR SUPPLY IS RIGHT IN FRONT OF YOU. BUT WHAT ABOUT WHEN THE NEXT PAYCHECK WON'T COVER IT? OR WHEN NO AMOUNT OF MONEY CAN BUY YOUR ANSWER?

Jezebel
POSSESSIONS OVER PEOPLE

Selections from 1 Kings 21

It's hard to relate to Jezebel— nauseated by the God of Israel and anyone who reminded her of him. But in this little episode, some of us must admit we see ourselves in her wicked eyes, worrying more about things than about people.

Ahab spoke to Naboth, saying, "Give me your vineyard." . . . However, Naboth said to Ahab, "I will absolutely not give my fathers' inheritance to you." So Ahab went to his palace sullen and seething. . . .

So [Jezebel] wrote letters in Ahab's name and sealed them with his seal. She sent the letters to the elders and nobles who lived with Naboth in his city. . . . Then they sent word to Jezebel, "Naboth has been stoned to death." . . . She said to Ahab, "Get up! Take possession of the vineyard of Naboth the Jezreelite who refused to give it to you for silver, for Naboth isn't alive, but dead."

Jezebel didn't do her own dirty work. She carefully stayed behind the scenes, putting up a show of innocence and unawareness while carving up Naboth for her own desires. It's the same thing we do sometimes—speaking politely to a person's face, waiting till they're out of earshot before we knife them in the back with gossip or shoot them with the daggers of our own thoughts. If we're to love people like we should, our hearts have to be as pleasant toward them as our appearances are. Otherwise, we're living a lie.

Look At It This Way

Anyone who says that money can't buy happiness has never bought new carpeting or a new car, or seen the look on a child's face on Christmas morning. The frustrating thing is that this kind of happiness is temporary. It always wears off. Desires once satisfied do not stay satisfied. That's how our minds and emotions work.

Contentment is a learned behavior, an acquired skill. It doesn't just happen when you fall into the right set of circumstances. Contentment cannot be purchased. And that's the best news, because it means that contentment is available to everyone, no matter what their financial situation might be.

Once you understand that fulfilling the desires of ego produces temporary satisfaction, and fulfilling the desires of your spirit brings lasting satisfaction, you can stop hoping to find lasting contentment in a new sofa. You will quit looking to material things to produce the contentment your spirit seeks. You will instinctively know the difference between momentary pleasure and deep-seated contentment. Contentment has a way of quieting insatiable desires.

—*Mary Hunt*

PEOPLE ARE AN ETERNAL INVESTMENT. IF YOUR POSSESSIONS ARE CONSUMING MORE OF YOUR TIME, THOUGHT, PRAYER, ENERGY, AND EFFORT THAN PEOPLE ARE, YOU'RE LIVING IN THE WRONG WORLD.

The Widow and the Oil
GOD WILL SUPPLY

Selections from 2 Kings 4

If you're familiar with the sinking feeling of rising debt, you know how this widow felt. She had scratched and clawed, only to barely survive. Now all the scratching and clawing in the world didn't matter. So she tried something new. She asked for help.

One of the wives of the sons of the prophets cried out to Elisha, "Your servant, my husband, has died. You know that your servant feared the LORD. Now the creditor is coming to take my two children as his slaves.". . .

Then [Elisha] said, "Go! Borrow empty vessels from everywhere—from all your neighbors.". . . They kept bringing her the vessels, and she kept pouring. When the vessels were full, she said to her son, "Bring me another vessel!" But he replied, "There aren't any more." Then the oil stopped. She went and told the man of God, who said, "Go sell the oil and pay your debt."

A young university president once went to the office of a wealthy businessman to ask for a donation to the school. "How much do you need?" the man offered. The rookie administrator threw out a figure. But as the businessman scrawled off a check for that exact amount, he said, "I want you to remember something. I'd have given you more if you had asked for it." God filled every container that the widow and her sons offered him. Wonder how much more oil he would have given if they had brought him more jars?

Look At It This Way

The widow of Second Kings 4 was absolutely desperate! As long as her husband lived, she trusted him as the source of all her need. Now desperation saw her without anyone to trust in but the Lord.

When this widow thought of her situation, all she could think of was a dead husband, an empty vessel, and a crowding creditor. She had not built up a memory bank of situations in which God had met her needs. When the man of God saw need and the end of human resources, he saw ravens, a barrel of meal which did not run out, and a cruse of oil whose supply did not cease. When he saw need, he saw the mighty hand of God. When she saw need, she saw panic. That is the difference between panic and praise.

There is nothing wrong with desperation if that desperation drives us to dependence upon God. The hope of our world lies in the fact that God is able! His ability can only be thrown into motion when we come to the end of our hoarded resources and put ourselves out upon God.

—*Jack Taylor*

WHEN ALL SEEMS HOPELESS, THINK BACK ON GOD'S SUPPLY. HAS HE EVER LEFT YOU WITHOUT ENOUGH? HAS HE EVER HELD BACK WHAT YOU REALLY NEEDED? HOLD OUT YOUR EMPTY JARS. AND TRUST HIM.

Shunammite Woman
PRACTICING HOSPITALITY

Selections from 2 Kings 4

The Shunam-mite woman had the time and money to be openly hospitable, you might say. She was a lady of leisure, with no kids, with few responsi-bilities. But does anybody ever have to go out of her way like this to make people feel welcome in her home? Do you?

One day Elisha went to Shunem. A prominent woman who lived there persuaded him to eat some food. . . . Then she said to her husband, "I know that the one who often passes by here is a holy man of God, so let's make a small upper room on the wall and put a bed, a table, a chair, and a lamp there for him. Whenever he comes, he can stay there."

One day he came there and stopped at the upper room to lie down. He ordered his servant Gehazi, "Call this Shunammite woman. . . . Say to her, 'Look, you've gone to all this trouble for us. What can we do for you?'"

There's only one way to "be hospitable . . . without complaining," as it says in First Peter 4:9. And that's to start with First Peter 4:8—"Above all, keep your love for one another at full strength." When we start by loving others, caring more about how we can serve, celebrate, and be an example of Christ by open-ing our homes and hearts to them, we'll be much less prone to resent the dusting and vacuuming or the money it costs. Some people come by hospitality nat-urally, but we can all grow into it with love.

Look At It This Way

Often we think of hospitality only as dinners and parties, but to be hospitable is to behave in a warm way and manner, to entertain with generous kindness. And a third thing for the Christian (not found in the dictionary) is that hospitality involves sensitivity and availability. If we are not sensitive to opportunities, then we are not available to them.

From time to time we all hurt. Every person who is honest enough to admit it will tell you that there are hurts that need the ministry of the Lord through God's people. Those who are not yet in the family of Christ need us to be his hands, his feet, his eyes, his ears, and his voice to help them find God's love.

There are times when we think, I don't want to be sweet perfume; I am too tired—too tired to behave in a warm manner to anyone who comes to my door today and needs to talk, too tired to entertain in a generous, kind way. We need to keep in mind God's economy, trusting him to supply our emotional and physical strength so that we can grasp the opportunities he sends our way.

—Doris Greig

OPENING YOURSELF TO THE MINISTRY OF HOSPITALITY MAY MEAN THAT PEOPLE WILL SEE WHAT'S IN YOUR CLOSETS AND UNDER YOUR BEDS. ISN'T IT WORTH IT, THOUGH, AS LONG AS THEY SEE WHAT'S IN YOUR HEART?

Naaman's Servant Girl
SERVING GOD

Selections from 2 Kings 5

During one of the frequent raids on Israel, a young girl had been captured and assigned to the household of Naaman, a commander in the Syrian army. Life as she had known it was over. But she was bent on show- ing her enemy that God's love was more than skin deep.

Naaman, commander of the army for the king of Aram, was a great man in his master's eyes and highly regarded because through him, the LORD had given victory to Aram. The man was a valiant warrior, but he had leprosy.

Aram had gone on raids and brought back from the land of Israel a young girl who served Naaman's wife. She said to her mistress, "If only my master would go to the prophet who is in Samaria! He would cure him of his leprosy."

So Naaman went and told his master what the girl from the land of Israel had said.

This nameless little servant girl stands tall in the pages of biblical history, because she was willing to bear witness for God in the midst of a foreign culture. Interestingly enough, today in America, individuals and families from many of the world's cultures are rapidly moving into our own neighborhoods, replanting their roots into the soil of freedom and opportunity. You may not have to look too many doors down to find someone who knows nothing about the love of Jesus Christ. Will you be the servant girl to point them to God?

Look At It This Way

When I went into teaching, I committed my work to the Lord. It seemed unreal, however, that our government, which had been formed on Christian principles, had ruled any form of religion out of the public schools. I wondered how it would be possible under the circumstances to fulfill my commitment. "Lord," I prayed, "show me how I can share Your love with my students when such a law exists."

The first fifteen minutes in the morning that had formerly been devoted to Bible reading, prayer, and reciting the Pledge of Allegiance became a time of inspirational readings, after which we would stand to salute the flag and bow our heads for a moment of reflection. I told the students that I liked to say a prayer to start the day, and suggested that maybe during that moment of silence, they would like to say one, too.

One day, one of my students asked if she could talk to me right after school. "Mrs. Anderson, would you pray for my grandma? She's awfully sick." It was then that I knew God had answered my prayer. In spite of the circumstances, he was still in control.

—*Gloria Anderson*

WHENEVER YOU FEEL AS THOUGH GOD HAS PASSED YOU BY, USING OTHERS TO DO BIG THINGS WHILE YOU'RE LEFT WITH THE ORDINARY, START LOOKING FOR WAYS TO SERVE HIM RIGHT WHERE YOU ARE.

Athaliah
GRASPING FOR POWER

Selections from 2 Kings 11

She was most likely the daughter of Ahab and Jezebel, if that gives you any clue as to how her character was molded. Born in power, raised in power, she never learned how to release power—and never learned that greatness finds those who aren't even seeking it.

Anointing [Joash], they clapped their hands, and said, "Long live the king!" When Athaliah heard the noise from the guard and the troops, she went to the troops in the LORD's temple. As she looked, there was the king standing by the pillar according to custom. The commanders and the trumpeters were by the king, and all the people of the land were rejoicing and blowing trumpets. Athaliah tore her clothes and screamed "Treason! Treason!"

Then Jehoiada the priest ordered the commanders of hundreds, those in charge of the army, "Take her out between the ranks, and put to death by the sword anyone who follows her."

Athaliah was the daughter of a king (Ahab), the sister of a king (Ahaziah of Israel), the wife of a king (Jehoram), and the mother of a king (Ahaziah of Judah). A little confusing, isn't it? She herself remained forever confused by her roles, never content being on the sidelines of power. That's why when her last grasp at royalty seemed at an end with her son's death, she killed all the grandsons she could get her hands on to claim the crown for herself. Isn't it shocking what a lust for power will make some people do?

Look At It This Way

Ask committed Christians if they understand that Jesus is the leader instead of them, and they will give you an odd look and say, "Well, of course Jesus is the leader." Yet if we believe this, why do we live as if we're in charge of our lives so much of the time?

On the surface, it sounds so simple: Jesus is the leader; we are the followers. But knowing that theological fact and living that discipleship truth are vastly different. As Christians, we should begin every day by affirming this truth: "Jesus is the leader; I am the follower. My goal today is to follow his schedule, accomplish his agenda, reach his destination, and love whoever he sends my way." That is true discipleship. Anything else is folly. As disciples, we should ask God to remind us every day how silly it is for us to think we are the leaders. Being the follower is a wonderful role, a role to celebrate, the role of a lifetime.

Live every day with that profound truth in mind, and you'll take a giant step forward in becoming a better follower of Jesus.

—John Kramp

MAINTAINING CONTROL OVER OURSELVES IS JOB ENOUGH WITHOUT NEEDING TO DOMINATE OTHERS. IF YOU'RE BATTLING ISSUES OF POWER AND CONTROL, CONFESS IT TODAY. TRUST GOD'S POWER TO HELP.

Jehoshabeath
HELPING HER OWN FAMILY

Selections from 2 Chronicles 22

Jehoshabeath would have been lost to the invisible pages of history— just another relative of royalty lost in the stream of unpronounceable names— had she not leapt to the defense of a one-year-old nephew and rescued her nation's kingly line from extermination.

When Jehu executed judgment on the house of Ahab, he found the rulers of Judah and the sons of Ahaziah's brothers who were serving Ahaziah, and he killed them. . . . So the house of Ahaziah had no one to exercise power over the kingdom.

When Athaliah, Ahaziah's mother, saw that her son was dead, she proceeded to persecute all the royal heirs of the house of Judah. Jehoshabeath, the king's daughter, stole Joash son of Ahaziah from among the king's sons who were being killed and put him and his nurse in a bedroom. . . . While Athaliah ruled over the land, he was hiding with them in God's temple for six years.

Christ himself came down hard against the people of his day—the self-righteously pious Pharisees—who shunned the genuine needs of their own families in order to make more showy contributions to the church. He knew that they—as we often are—were inherently drawn to acts of charity that yielded more noticeable, immediate, and self-gratifying returns than did the slow-moving, unadvertised sacrifices of tending to family matters. Giving unselfishly to our own families tests the true heart of a servant of God.

Look At It This Way

One night, our sisters went out to pick up the people on the streets. They saw a young man there late at night, lying in the street, and they said, "You should not be here; you should be with your parents." And he said, "When I go home, my mother does not want me because I have long hair. Every time I go home, she pushes me out." By the time they came back, he had taken an overdose, and they had to take him to the hospital.

I could not help thinking it was quite possible his mother was busy, with the hunger of our people in India, and there was her own child hungry for her, hungry for her love, hungry for her care, and she refused it.

It is easy to love the people far away. It is not always easy to love those close to us. It is easier to give a cup of rice to relieve hunger than to relieve the loneliness and pain of someone unloved in our own home. Bring love into your home, for this is where our love for each other must start.

—Mother Teresa

HAVE YOU EVER BEEN SHORT WITH YOUR CHILD OR HUSBAND, ONLY TO BE INTERRUPTED BY A CALL FROM A LITTLE-KNOWN ACQUAINTANCE WHO SUDDENLY GOT YOUR KIND AND FULL ATTENTION? WHY DO WE DO THAT?

Huldah
SPEAKING GOD'S TRUTH

Selections from 2 Chronicles 34

Huldah became a sought-after sage when the old scrolls of Scripture were found under decades of dust. Watch her straight-forward way of speaking truth into a difficult situation, and see if it can teach us anything about how to confront our trouble spots.

When the king heard the words of the law, he tore his clothes. Then he commanded . . . "Go. Inquire of the LORD for me and for those remaining in Israel and Judah, concerning the words of the book that was found. For great is the LORD's wrath that is poured out on us because our fathers have not kept the word of the LORD." . . .

Those the king had designated went to the prophetess Huldah. . . . She said to them . . . "This is what the LORD says: 'I am about to bring disaster on this place and on its inhabitants, fulfilling all the curses written in the book that they read.'"

Like Isaiah, Jeremiah, and her other contemporaries in the prophecy field during these lean years in Hebrew history, Huldah had probably logged many hours railing her unwelcome truths into the hostile air of idolatry and rebellion. But read on in Second Chronicles 34 and notice that even as she prophesies punishment, her message is tinged with mercy. In so doing, she shines a light into the heart of God, revealing him again as a God who rages at sin, but mainly because it blinds human eyes to his redemption.

Look At It This Way

Confrontation is tricky. We all have logs in our own eyes, so it seems a bit presumptuous to go after the speck in our sister's eye. Yet Solomon tells us, "Better is open rebuke than hidden love" (Proverbs 27:5, NIV) and "Faithful are the wounds of a friend" (Proverbs 27:6, NASB). So there is a time for confrontation, but it should pass a few tests.

First, our motive for confrontation should be changed behavior rather than the release of our anger. If the person is unlikely to respond, why do it? Next, be sure your anger is healed. Otherwise, confrontation is likely to be misinterpreted as a personal attack rather than an effort to improve the relationship.

Our motivation for confrontation should always spring from a desire to improve the relationship or seek the other person's best. If we confront just to release anger, we destroy rather than build up. Most of us can tell whether we are being confronted in order to help, in a spirit of genuine love and good will, or whether the confrontation is intended to hurt or destroy. A mature rose can usually handle the shock of loving confrontation from a close friend.

—Dee Brestin

IF YOU'RE FACING AN INEVITABLE "SPEAKING THE TRUTH IN LOVE" CONFRONTATION WITH A BOSS, FRIEND, OR SOMEONE IN YOUR FAMILY, REMEMBER YOUR GOLDEN RULE COMMISSION TO LEAD WITH GRACE AND MERCY.

Vashti
STRONG OR STUBBORN?

Selections from Esther 1

Xerxes was a real jerk. The very idea of demanding that his wife parade in front of a bunch of drunken dignitaries! And watching them scramble to make sense of her refusal is downright hilarious. Submission doesn't mean you'll do just anything.

The king ordered them to bring Queen Vashti before him with her royal crown to show off her beauty to the people and to the officials, since she was stunning. Queen Vashti refused to come. . . . The king exploded, his anger blazing within him. . . .

"Queen Vashti has defied not only the king, but all the officials and all the peoples who are in every one of King Xerxes's provinces. For this incident with the queen will become public knowledge to all women and cause them to despise their husbands. They will justify this by saying, 'King Xerxes ordered Queen Vashti brought before him, but she didn't come.'"

*B*efore we get too carried away with all this in-your-face independence, let's remember that a wife's freedom to stand on principle against her husband's abuse, immorality, or unethical behavior is much different than getting in the habit of rejecting his opinions just because you don't agree with them. Who knows but that it wasn't unlike Vashti to thumb her nose at just about anything Xerxes asked? Submission is not a ball and chain that strips you of all self-defense. But it *is* meant to strip away our selfishness.

Look At It This Way

Tim was a devout Christian trying to build his new marriage on biblical principles, and he wanted to be the "head" of the home—"The husband is the head of the wife as Christ is the head of the church" (Ephesians 5:23, NIV). Tim interpreted this statement to mean that it was his job to be the boss of his wife. And it was her job to be submissive to his demands. Tim's wife, however, didn't see things that way because she lived in the twentieth century, not the first. She saw herself, understandably, as an equal partner in the marriage.

It never seemed to occur to Tim that in the Bible, the husband is never called to make his wife submit. The Bible doesn't call husbands to rule over their wives, but to renounce the desire to be master. Out of reverence for Christ, husbands should be the first to honor and respect their wives.

A healthy marriage is built on a mutual desire to submit one's needs to the other. Without mutual submission, every marriage will eventually falter. The key is understanding that submission in marriage is a two-way street.

—*Les Parrott*

OUR FIRST CALLING IN LIFE IS TO SUBMIT OURSELVES TO GOD. BUT HE HAS GIVEN US TO EACH OTHER TO SHOW US WHAT SUBMISSION REALLY COSTS. ASK YOURSELF IF YOU'RE SUBMITTED TO YOUR HUSBAND.

Esther
RESPECTING AUTHORITY

Selections from Esther 2

Give us enough pampering, attention, and pats on the back, and pretty soon we get to thinking we're a little better than we really are, a little smarter than everyone else. Or if we're smart like Esther, we still realize that there's wisdom in years.

When Esther's turn came to go to the king (she was the daughter of Abihail, who was the uncle of Mordecai, the man who had adopted her as his daughter), she didn't ask for anything except what Hegai, the king's trusted official in charge of the harem, suggested. Esther won approval in the eyes of everyone who gazed upon her. . . .

When the young women were assembled together for a second time . . . Esther still had not revealed her birthplace or her ethnic background, just as Mordecai had directed. Esther obeyed Mordecai's orders just as she had while he raised her.

*M*ost of us have lived long enough now to know that the roles played by people in authority are not as easy as they seemed from down below. Now that we are the parents, supervisors, managers, and coordinators, we understand that those jobs come complete with unforeseen challenges and complexities. So as we respond to those who remain in authority over us at this stage of life—pastors, bosses, and others—let's help them do their jobs better by not being catty and cynical, serving them the way we'd like to be served.

Look At It This Way

Think of it: no job, no responsibility, no cooking, no clean-up, no washing, no ironing, no errands, no budget-watching, no holding back in any area. All of the emphasis rests upon her becoming a woman of greater physical beauty. Jewelry, clothing, perfumes, cosmetics, whatever she wishes, from coiffure to pedicure, are hers. The only thing on everyone's mind is to win the contest—to please the king and gain his favor.

Remember, at this time, Esther cannot be more than twenty years old or so, and she could have been younger. This is a chance of a lifetime for her to have whatever she wishes. Instead, she remains true to what she has been taught and abides by the counsel of Mordecai, believing that he knows what is best for her. She does not succumb to the temptation around her—the superficiality, the selfishness, the seduction, the self-centeredness. She displays an unselfish modesty and authenticity amid unparalleled extravagance. She knew who she was. She knew what she believed. And she knew that God's hand was on her life.

—*Charles Swindoll*

YOU CAN'T PICK ALL YOUR AUTHORITY FIGURES. BUT HAVE YOU THOUGHT ABOUT CHOOSING ONE OR TWO WHO ARE WILLING TO INVEST THEMSELVES IN YOUR LIFE, PEOPLE YOU CAN TRUST TO ADVISE YOU WELL?

Esther
SEEKING GOD
THROUGH FASTING

Selections from Esther 4

A nation is
on the brink
of extinction.
Every avenue
has been tried,
every appeal
squashed.
Now it's
down to one
woman with
the longest of
long shots in
front of her. If
there's to be
any hope, if
there's to be
any chance,
the people
must fast.
And pray.

Mordecai told the messenger to reply to Esther . . . "If you keep silent at this time, liberation and deliverance will arise for the Jewish people from another place, but you and your father's house will be destroyed. Who knows, but that you have attained your royal position for such a time as this?"

Esther told the messenger to reply to Mordecai, "Go, assemble all the Jews who can be found in Susa and fast on my behalf. Don't eat or drink for three days, night and day. I and my maidservants will also fast in the same way. Having done this, I will go to the king even if it is against the law. If I perish, I perish."

Our lives have become so noisy and complicated that it's hard to keep our minds on one thought for very long. That's why many times when we sit down to pray, we can look up ten minutes later only to find that we've mostly been thinking about the movie we watched on TV last night or how we're going to get to the cleaners this afternoon before they close. One of the benefits of fasting is to clear our head, free up our time, and get our spirit quiet enough to really talk—and really listen—to God.

Look At It This Way

The discipline of fasting challenges us in an area where our culture is often the most undisciplined. One of the great obsessions of Western culture is eating. Whether for the pure sensual pleasure of the task or as a replacement for the emotional nurture we do not receive, overeating or starving are struggles many women and men face. Fasting challenges us to be disciplined in our eating and drinking.

Traditionally, the fast was implemented to elicit God's support, to change his mind concerning judgment, to understand what is confusing in one's personal circumstances, and to gain wisdom for making decisions. The fast also is used to petition God regarding resolutions for the problems of society and for ways to overcome our own weaknesses. The fast is also adopted to seek forgiveness on behalf of a group or for our nation's behavior.

Finally, fasting is to honor and glorify God. It is designed to draw us into knowing God more fully, to learn his ways rather than only petitioning to gain our own way. Esther sought wisdom through active waiting while she fasted and withdrew into solitude.

—Normajean Hinders

FASTING IS ONE OF THE FORGOTTEN DISCIPLINES IN MANY CHRISTIANS' LIVES. YES, YOU WILL GET HUNGRY. BUT YOU MAY FIND "FOOD TO EAT THAT YOU DON'T KNOW ABOUT" (JOHN 4:32).

Esther
USING HER INFLUENCE

Selections from Esther 8

In Esther, we see a young girl growing in her understanding of what God had placed her in high places to do. And part of her maturity came from knowing when to speak, when to wait, and how to work within the system without sacrificing her integrity.

[Esther] said, "If I have found approval before the king, if the matter seems right to him, and if I am pleasing in his sight, may a royal edict be written. Let it revoke the documents that the scheming Haman son of Hammedatha the Agagite, wrote to destroy the Jews who reside in all the king's provinces. For how could I bear to witness the evil that would come on my people? How could I endure if I witness the destruction of my relatives?"

King Xerxes said to Esther the Queen . . . "Write in the king's name whatever pleases you concerning the Jews. Seal it with the royal signet ring."

From the glimpses we get of Esther, she doesn't appear to be the type of woman who was dead set on storming the castle with her own reforms. Each time she takes a stand before the king, you get the feeling her hands are sweating, her pulse is racing. She halfway wishes she had never gotten herself into this spot in the first place. But marshaling every ounce of courage, she softly strides in, timidly opens her mouth, and surprises even herself by the boldness with which she speaks. This is not like her. This is like . . . God.

Look At It This Way

When the women of a country are lulled into apathy and lack of concern for the welfare of their nation, the condition is tragic indeed. However, we can hear the prophet of old, through whom the Lord speaks to us today. We can arise and do the very opposite of what we have been doing. We can rebuke our lethargy and indifference and change our attitudes. We can awaken and act!

Here is our game plan: (1) Pray as you have never prayed before for our country and for the people who have the power to change its direction; (2) Inform yourself by reading, listening, and observing, and seek counsel from godly people who are informed about the state of our nation; (3) Enlist other women to stand with you in a renewed commitment to meaningful citizenship; (4) Vote in elections on every level.

Citizenship and its duties are God-given responsibilities which are not optional or transferrable. Women, we can make a difference in calling our nation back to God!

—Dorothy Kelley Patterson

YOUR EXPERIENCE, KNOWLEDGE, AND GIFTINGS HAVE PLACED YOU IN A UNIQUE POSITION TO MAKE AN IMPACT ON SOMEBODY, SOMEWHERE. HAVE YOU DISCOVERED WHERE YOU WERE MEANT TO SERVE?

Job's Wife
NAGGING HER HUSBAND

You can't fault Job's wife for being upset. They had just lost everything. But instead of sitting down with Job, drawing comfort together in their shared misery, his wife pointed a finger at his character. And at God. And that's where she went wrong.

"Have you considered My servant, Job?" the LORD inquired of the Adversary, "No one else on earth is like him. He maintains his integrity, is upright, fears God, and turns away from evil."...

The Adversary left the LORD's presence. He struck Job with severe sores from the bottom of his foot to the top of his head. Job took a broken piece of pottery to scrape himself while he sat among the ashes. "Are you still holding on to your integrity?" his wife demanded of him. "Curse God and die!"

He scolded her, "Shall we accept the good from God but not accept the evil?"

Whenever you resort to nagging, it means you've let your anger and frustration obscure your view of two things you know to be true. First, you can't really change your husband—only God can. And second, nagging doesn't work even if you *could* change him. How many times has he responded to your rantings with, "You know what, honey? You're right. I am a big buffoon. How could I not have seen it before?" Nearly never. A better response is always prayer, teamed with your best attempts at confronting him in love.

Look At It This Way

I have always prided myself on being a good wife. Be unfaithful to my husband? I wouldn't even think of it! Neglect him? Not me! I carefully prepare healthful, tasty meals every day. I keep his clothes washed and ironed, the house clean and neat. But I have discovered that there is more than one way to tear down a marriage. Some do it in one fell swoop by asking for a divorce. Some of us do it in little bits and pieces.

"Honey, I put those paper towels in your bathroom so you can wipe the splashes off your mirror." (Why doesn't he remember? It would just take a second!)

"Aren't you going to get into the right lane? We have to turn pretty soon, you know." (Why doesn't he drive like I do?)

"Why are we taking this route to church today? Don't you think the other way is faster?" (I know the other way is better.)

Tearing down—one little piece at a time, disapproving, criticizing, nagging. Water, over a period of time, wears away even stone. What is my constant dripping doing to my marriage?

—*Matilda Nordtvedt*

NEXT TIME YOU'RE TEMPTED TO FUSS ABOUT YOUR HUSBAND'S HABITS AND HANG-UPS, TURN HIM OVER TO GOD IN PRAYER. JUST BE SURE TO GIVE GOD PERMISSION TO MAKE SOME CHANGES IN YOU, TOO.

The Wise Mother
TEACHING HER CHILDREN

Selections from Proverbs 1, 2, 6

The goal in teaching and disciplining our children is not so they can behave in the checkout line, but so they can become so accustomed to obeying us while they're under our wing, they'll have no problem obeying God when they're out on their own.

Don't reject your mother's teaching, for [it] will be a garland of grace on your head and a gold chain around your neck. . . . Then you will understand righteousness, justice, and integrity—every good path. For wisdom will enter your heart, and knowledge will delight your soul. Discretion will watch over you, and understanding will guard you. . . .

When you walk here and there, they will guide you; when you lie down, they will watch over you; when you wake up, they will talk to you. For a commandment is a lamp, teaching is a light, and corrective instructions are the way to life.

We always need to be on the lookout for those teachable moments with our children—spontaneous lessons that appear in the side yard, the laundry room, the grocery store. But those are not really enough, because anything that we relegate to haphazard status will often get crowded out of our schedules. If it's important to us, then sitting down with our children on a regular basis to listen, ask questions, share our hearts, search the Scriptures, or talk things over with God is worth the extra commitment.

Look At It This Way

It is easier to talk about issues like servanthood, humility, and obedience than it is to make them a reality in the lives of our children. We know that it is not enough for us to memorize the meaning of these words; we must live them out in our actions.

It can be difficult to teach these qualities when we know that we are in our own lives still struggling to learn these Christlike qualities. As parents, we may lack the confidence to teach characteristics that we know we fail to carry out as we should, or we fear that we will be exposed as hypocrites in the eyes of our own children.

But we must remember that it is only by the Lord's grace that we are qualified to be his representatives and to bear the responsibility of training our children in his likeness. If we abandon this vision because of our fear, then we are left to wander aimlessly with no direction other than our own self-interest. It is far better that we admit our frequent failings and still keep our eyes focused on the race we are called to run.

—Susan Card

TRUTH IS, YOU'RE TEACHING YOUR CHILDREN SOMETHING EVERY MINUTE YOU'RE AROUND THEM. MAKE SURE THE THINGS YOU'RE DOING ARE LINING UP WITH THE THINGS YOU'RE SAYING.

The Virtuous Woman
MAKING FAMILY TOP PRIORITY

Selections from Proverbs 31

Just when you thought you'd seen the last of that Proverbs 31 woman, here she comes again to remind you how wonderful she is. But don't look at her as someone who is larger than life. See in her all the things you can become with the help of Almighty God.

Who can find a capable wife? She is far more precious than jewels. The heart of her husband trusts in her, and he will not lack anything good. She rewards him with good, not evil, all the days of her life. . . . She rises while it is still night and provides food for her household and portions for her servants. . . . She makes her own bed coverings; her clothing is fine linen and purple.

Her husband is known at the city gates, where he sits among the elders of the land. . . . Her sons rise up and call her blessed. Her husband also praises her: "Many women are capable, but you surpass them all!"

You've probably never been this busy before. And on top of the tasks that are right in front of you are dozens of others you don't have time for—things you'd do if you could. It means having to make constant between work and church and friends and . . . everything. But in all your choices, make sure you're giving your family your best. Some of those other things may not get done. Someone else may have to take your place. But no one can take your place at home. You're the only one who can do what you do.

Look At It This Way

The Proverbs 31 woman is a far cry from many of her twentieth-century sisters. The annals of business are filled with stories of women who are stressed out, overworked, and absent from home. Unfortunately, since many of these women are also wives and mothers, their families are paying a terrible price.

Obviously, the culture of Proverbs 31 is also a far cry from modern times. This woman worked out of her home, so she was also available to her family. Many people would say that the "ideal" isn't possible today. But more and more women are finding creative ways to carry on their outside work while being at home.

The writer of Proverbs 31 never says that we need to be merchants, expert seamstresses, real estate buyers, or market traders to be women of nobility. This particular woman had these abilities, but they may not be your areas of expertise. The principle of the Scripture is that the wise use of your gifts qualifies you for the title of noble wife. Many women will say that their commitment to the Lord, to their husbands, and to their children is the way they maximize their gifts.

—*Lois Evans*

JESUS TALKED ABOUT THE COSTLY TRADE-OFF BETWEEN GAINING THE WHOLE WORLD BUT LOSING OUR OWN SOULS. WE CAN LOSE OUR FAMILIES, TOO, IF WE LOSE OUR FOCUS ON WHO COMES FIRST.

The Virtuous Woman
WE'LL MANAGE

Selections from Proverbs 31

Like us, the Proverbs 31 woman went to bed feeling exhausted, knowing she'd be waking up to do the same thing again tomorrow. Work can certainly take a lot out of us, but when we do it for God, he can do a lot with us. Isn't that what we're working for?

She selects wool and flax and works with willing hands. She is like the merchant ships, bringing her food from far away. . . .

She evaluates a field and buys it; she plants a vineyard with her earnings. She draws on her strength and reveals that her arms are strong.

She sees that her profits are good, and her lamp never goes out at night. She extends her hands to the spinning staff, and her hands hold the spindle. . . .

She watches over the activities of her household, and she is never idle.

Let's face it. We'll never get to read all the books we want, or go on all the walks we want, or watch every old rerun we want. And we already know why —because we've got work to do. And since that's the case, we can either keep our minds on what we're missing, adding even more weight to the work in front of us, or we can keep our heads in what we're doing— finding joy in simple things, seeing opportunity in ordinary tasks, discovering a new side of God in our mundane moments.

Look At It This Way

I would love to meet the woman described in Proverbs 31. I didn't always feel so kindly toward her. As I've changed, however, I've changed my mind about her too. I'm not sure I'll ever equal her amazing abilities, but she certainly sets an example well worth emulating.

She is resourceful, entrepreneurial, and a financial wizard. Did you notice how she buys land, plants a vineyard, and then knows when to sell? She doesn't mortgage her husband's future by getting into all kinds of debt that will keep them in bondage for years to come. She doesn't think it's her job to spend and his job to provide. Let me tell you, if she had $100,000 in unsecured debt breathing down her neck with a drawer full of bills she's afraid her husband might find, cheerful would not be one of the ways her children described her. Her husband and kids are proud of her, which doesn't surprise me one bit.

There is absolutely no question in my mind that God honors this kind of pursuit and has given her profile to us as an example, a standard, an ideal.

—*Mary Hunt*

HOW ARE YOU APPROACHING THE WORK THAT GOD HAS GIVEN YOU TO DO? WITH BITTERNESS? OR WITH THANKFULNESS? WITH A SIGH? OR WITH A SMILE? LIFE TAKES WORK, BUT HAPPINESS TAKES A GOOD ATTITUDE.

The Virtuous Woman
SELFLESS SERVICE

Selections from Proverbs 31

This noble example of godly living offers another sterling quality to admire and acquire— a willingness to pour her heart out for others, to see that those within her reach are fed with whatever God enables her to provide. She's really something. So are you.

Her hands reach out to the poor, and she extends her hands to the needy. She is not afraid for her household when it snows, for all in her household are doubly clothed. . . .

She makes and sells linen garments; she delivers belts to the merchants. Strength and honor are her clothing, and she can laugh at the time to come. She opens her mouth with wisdom, and loving instruction is on her tongue. . . .

Charm is deceptive and beauty is fleeting, but a woman who fears the Lord will be praised. Give her the reward of her labor, and let her works praise her at the city gates.

All this talk about doing and giving is what most of us need to hear—most of the time. But perhaps you need to hear the other side of that story— that you can't give what you don't have, and that you needn't feel guilty every time you enjoy a wholesome pleasure or soak in a hot tub bath until your toes prune up. Sometimes, doing too many acts of service can throw you off balance—burning you out or feeding an unhealthy desire to be recognized. Sometimes, it's *you* that needs a little nourishment and taking care of.

Look At It This Way

"I don't have time" is probably a lie more often than not, covering "I don't want to." We have time—twenty-four hours in a day, seven days in a week. Demands on our time differ, of course, and it is here that the disciple must refer to her Master. *What do you want me to do, Lord?*

There were endless demands on Jesus' time. Still he was able to make that amazing claim of "completing the work you gave me to do" (John 17:4, NIV). This was not the same as saying he had finished everything he could possibly think of to do, or that he had done everything others had asked. The claim was that he had done what had been given.

The work of God is appointed. There is always enough time to do the will of God. For that, we can never say, "I don't have time." When we find ourselves frantic and frustrated, harried and harassed, it is a sign that we are running on our own schedule, not on God's. Frustration is not the will of God. There is time to do anything and everything that God wants us to do.

—*Elisabeth Elliot*

THE GREATEST JOY IN ALL THE WORLD IS OBEYING CHRIST BY SERVING OTHERS. IF YOU'RE FEELING ABSORBED IN YOUR OWN PROBLEMS AND PRESSURES, DO SOMETHING SPECIAL FOR SOMEONE ELSE.

Solomon's Lover
SEEKING INTIMACY

Selections from Song of Solomon 4

There are many days when you wake up feeling like anything but an incense tree or a garden of savory spices. But maybe that's because you've never really been able to believe just how much God loves you. He thinks you're beautiful just the way you are.

How beautiful you are, my darling. How very beautiful! Behind your veil, your eyes are doves. . . . You are absolutely beautiful, my darling, with no imperfection in you. . . . You have captured my heart, my sister, my bride. You have captured my heart with one glance of your eyes, with one jewel of your necklace.

How delightful your love is, my sister, my bride. Your love is much better than wine, and the fragrance of your perfume than any balsam. Your lips drip sweetness like the honeycomb, my bride. Honey and milk are under your tongue. The fragrance of your garments is like the fragrance of Lebanon.

*B*ringing up the subject of intimacy usually causes us to dodge, to dart our eyes, and become extremely interested in discussing the unusual weather we're having for this time of year. But underneath our avoidance of vulnerability, we know that the struggles we face in the intimacy department are primarily spiritual ones. The marriage relationship so closely resembles Christ's desire for his church, we should never be surprised that a breakdown in communion with him results in a meltdown of our comfort with closeness.

Look At It This Way

We understand this sacred love-song to be a Canticle of Communion between the Lord Jesus Christ and his church. He is the Bridegroom, and she is the bride. See how near, how dear, thou art to him! Though he is Master and Lord, yet it is such a loving lordship which he exercises towards us that we rejoice in it. When we bow before him, it is not because we fear with servile trembling, but because we rejoice and love. We rejoice in his rule and reign. Perfect love hath cast out fear. We live in such a joyful fellowship with him as a sister with a brother, or a wife with a husband.

Be not backward towards your own betrothed. Be not stiff and cold. Set not a bound about the mount, for it is not Sinai—there are no bounds to the hill of Zion. Hang not up a curtain, for he has rent the veil. Think not of him as though he were far divided from you, for he is exceeding near to you and has taken you up unto himself, to be one with him forever.

—*Charles Spurgeon*

HOW ARE YOU TWO GROWING CLOSER TO EACH OTHER SPIRITUALLY? DON'T WASTE YOUR TIME FEELING GUILTY ABOUT IT. YOU'RE IN VERY GOOD COMPANY. BUT ISN'T THIS A GOOD DAY TO START CHANGING ALL THAT?

Mary
SAYING YES

Selections from Luke 1

Try reading this passage, not in the light of Christmas, but in the darkness of the years before it. Put yourself in the room with Mary. Listen to what the angel is asking her to believe. Would you be afraid? Yes. Upset? Yes. Would you be able to say . . . yes?

The angel Gabriel was sent by God . . . to a virgin engaged to a man named Joseph. . . . "Now listen: You will conceive and give birth to a son, and you will call His name JESUS.". . .

Mary asked the angel, "How can this be, since I have not been intimate with a man?" The angel replied to her: "The Holy Spirit will come upon you, and the power of the Most High will overshadow you. Therefore the holy child to be born will be called the Son of God. . . . For nothing will be impossible with God."

"Consider me the Lord's slave," said Mary. "May it be done to me according to your word."

How do we know whether something we've seen, felt, or heard is really from God? What proof did Mary have once her eyes readjusted to the now dim-looking sunlight, once her heart rate slowed down, once the boom of the angel's voice gave way to the whistle of a songbird? Nothing—except a pretty good hunch. But as she waited, little things began to happen. Waves of morning sickness. Jabs and kicks from her womb that awakened her in the night. When it's God, the proof keeps coming, as we watch and wait.

Look At It This Way

He found the little dull town, the dusty street, the right house. In obedience, he went in, stood before the astonished girl, and spoke. An angel's voice, speaking in the accents of Nazareth.

Mary was not a feeble girl—weak and without spunk, imagination, or initiative. Subsequent action proves that. But she was meek. Never confuse weak with meek. She was meek as Moses was meek—strong and holy enough to recognize her place under God. Thoughts of what people would say, what Joseph would say, or how she would ever convince them that she had not been unfaithful were instantly set aside.

Mission accomplished, the angel left her. Back he flies, past Mars, Jupiter, Saturn, Uranus, beyond the Southern Cross and the Milky Way, and finally to the firmament of his native world where the will of the God of all those heavens and firmaments is always done, and always done perfectly. He brought back a message: On that planet, in Galilee, in a town called Nazareth, in the house to which God had sent him, the girl named Mary had said yes.

—*Elisabeth Elliot*

THE WHOLE PREMISE OF CHRISTIANITY IS BEYOND UNDERSTANDING—A GOD WHO BECAME MAN, A MAN WHO BECAME OUR PERFECT SACRIFICE. DO WE ALWAYS HAVE TO UNDERSTAND IN ORDER TO OBEY?

Mary
POURING FORTH PRAISE

Selections from Luke 1

Her first thought at having heard the impossible report of the angel may have been disbelief. Her first reaction may have been to try figuring out how to tell her parents and fiancé. We don't know. But we know her first words were words of praise.

Mary said: "My soul proclaims the greatness of the Lord, and my spirit has rejoiced in God my Savior, because He has looked with favor on the humble condition of His slave. Surely, from now on all generations will call me blessed, because the Mighty One has done great things for me, and holy is His name.

"His mercy is from generation to generation on those who fear Him. He has done a mighty deed with His arm; He has scattered the proud because of the thoughts of their hearts; He has toppled the mighty from their thrones and exalted the lowly. He has satisfied the hungry with good things and sent the rich away empty."

*W*hen was the last time you found a place to yourself, turned off the radio and the television, closed your door to the world around you, and opened your mouth in unharnessed praise—just letting the words of worship and thanks tumble out of your heart, allowing God to fill in the gaps with long-forgotten blessings and fresh, new dimensions of his goodness and love? Like Mary, you'll find your soul—your very will—wanting to worship, choosing to cherish him. And your spirit rejoicing that he has set you free.

Look At It This Way

Mary was overwhelmed by the Lord's goodness to her. In response, she sang one of the most beautiful and profound songs of praise found in Scripture. Trying to stop the praise of a thankful heart would be like trying to arrest the flow of a mighty waterfall! God created us to praise him; praise will be our activity when we are gathered around his throne in heaven.

You should never have difficulty thinking of reasons why God deserves your praise. You should enjoy the times you have to praise your Lord, both privately and publicly in worship. If your life is not filled with praise, it may be that you have lost your appreciation for God's merciful activity in your life.

Never forget what God has saved you from. Never take for granted what it means to have the assurance of eternity with God. Do not disregard the spiritual kinship you enjoy with other believers. Take time often to recount the blessings he has poured out upon you and your family. As you contemplate the boundless love and mercy God has shown you, you will want to sing his praises as Mary did.

—*Henry Blackaby*

WORSHIP IS A HABIT, AN EXERCISE—A CHOICE TO REORDER THE WAY YOU THINK AND LIVE, CLAIMING GODLY PRAISE AS YOUR TOP PRIORITY— WORSHIPING AT WILL, AT A MOMENT'S NOTICE, AT ALL TIMES.

Mary

INSIDE KNOWLEDGE

Selections from Luke 2

To know what Mary knew, but to try not showing Jesus favoritism over her other children. To bite her tongue when mothers talked about the great things their kids would do someday. Every mother encounters new thoughts and feelings. But can you imagine hers?

Every year His parents traveled to Jerusalem for the Passover Festival. . . . As they were returning, the boy Jesus stayed behind in Jerusalem, but His parents did not know it. . . . After three days, they found Him in the temple complex sitting among the teachers, listening to them and asking them questions. . . .

His mother said to Him, "Son, why have You treated us like this? Your father and I have been anxiously searching for You."

"Why were you searching for Me?" He asked them. "Didn't you know that I must be involved in my Father's interests?". . .

His mother kept all these things in her heart.

As Christians, we all live with inside knowledge—an awareness that God is ultimately in control, that he has his hand upon us, that he has a plan for our lives. But many times, the specific steps for following that plan aren't spelled out right in front of us. That's when we can relate with the psalmist who wrote, "When I tried to understand all this, it seemed hopeless until I entered God's sanctuary. Then I understood" (Psalm 73:16-17). In his presence, we find the strength to go on—whether we have knowledge or not.

Look At It This Way

We see nothing of her for twelve years—days and nights, weeks and months, years and years of caring for the infant, the toddler, the little boy, the adolescent. Mary has no witness, no limelight, no special recognition of any kind. She is not Mother of the Year. She was content to be silent before God.

Hers was a hidden life, a faithful one, a holy one—holy in the context of a humble home in a small village where there was not very much diversion. She knew that the ordinary duties were ordained for her as much as the extraordinary way in which they became her assignment. She struck no poses. She was the mother of a baby, willing to be known simply as his mother for the rest of her life. He was an extraordinary baby, the Eternal Word, but his needs were very ordinary, very daily, to his mother.

I thank him for her silence. I want to learn what she had learned so early: the deep guarding in her heart of each event, mulling over its meaning from God, waiting in silence for his word to her.

—*Evelyn Christenson*

ONE OF THE BEST WAYS TO KEEP YOUR AWARENESS OF GOD'S PLAN IN MIND AND TO WATCH IT UNFOLD LITTLE BY LITTLE IN YOUR LIFE IS THROUGH THE DISCIPLINE OF JOURNALING. TRY IT FOR A WHILE AND SEE.

Mary
ON GOOD TERMS WITH GOD

Mary's words seem almost forward, as though she thinks she somehow knows better than Jesus does how to initiate his own ministry. Or are we instead witnessing what happens when a person knows Jesus so well, she almost begins thinking like him?

On the third day a wedding took place in Cana of Galilee. Jesus' mother was there, and Jesus and His disciples were invited to the wedding as well. When the wine ran out, Jesus' mother told Him, "They don't have any wine."

"What has this concern of yours to do with Me, woman?" Jesus asked. "My hour has not yet come."

"Do whatever He tells you," His mother told the servants. . . . And they did. . . . When the chief servant tasted the water (after it had become wine), he did not know where it came from—though the servants who had drawn the water knew.

$\mathcal{D}$o you think we'd know Jesus better if—as Mary and his closest friends did—we could actually sit down next to him and warm ourselves by the fire, if we could catch him on his way to the seashore and ask if we could come along, if we could hear him sharing his puzzlingly wise answers over punch glasses at a wedding reception? We actually have more time with him right now than any of those did who had but three short years to look into his eyes and recognize his engaging voice. He's waiting. . . . Where are we?

Look At It This Way

We can state the gospel clearly; we can smell unsound doctrine a mile away. If asked how one may come to know God, we can at once produce the right formula: that we come to know God through Jesus Christ the Lord, in virtue of his cross and mediation, on the basis of his word of promise, by the power of the Holy Spirit, via a personal exercise of faith. Yet the gaiety, goodness, and unfetteredness of spirit which are the marks of those who have known God are rare among us—rarer, perhaps, than they are in some other Christian circles where, by comparison, evangelical truth is less clearly and fully known.

Interest in theology, and knowledge about God, and the capacity to think clearly and talk well on Christian themes, is not at all the same thing as knowing him. One can have all this and hardly know God at all. The question is not whether we are good at theology. The question is, can we say simply, honestly—not because we feel that as evangelicals we ought to, but because it is a plain matter of fact—that we have known God?

—*J. I. Packer*

THINK OF THE THINGS THAT YOU ALLOW TO STAND IN YOUR WAY FROM BEING ALONE WITH JESUS— FROM PRAYING, WAITING, LEARNING HOW TO LISTEN. ARE THEY REALLY WORTH THE BLESSINGS YOU'RE GIVING UP?

Mary
FAITHFUL TO THE END

We've grown so accustomed to seeing her as a teenage mother that we struggle to see her in black, in shock, in dazed tearfulness, looking much older than her 45, 50 years. When she had found favor with God, he was looking at this part of her life too.

They took Jesus away. Carrying His own cross, He went out to what is called Skull Place, which in Hebrew is called Golgotha. There they crucified Him and two others with Him, one on either side, with Jesus in the middle. . . .

Standing by the cross of Jesus were His mother, His mother's sister, Mary the wife of Clopas, and Mary Magdalene. When Jesus saw His mother and the disciple He loved standing there, He said to His mother, "Woman, here is your son." Then He said to the disciple, "Here is your mother." And from that hour the disciple took her into his home.

Mary had watched so patiently from the sidelines. She had seen Jesus degraded by the religious establishment she'd been taught to respect. She'd been ridiculed by townspeople eager to seek holes in her heavenly story. Her own boys—his brothers—didn't even believe in him. And if she were totally honest with herself, there were times when even she wondered if he was stepping over the line. But still, she finds herself here, at the base of a cross. What else is a mother to do? Even though he's God's Son, he's still her little boy.

Look At It This Way

When Sorrow sang, her notes were like the low, sweet call of the nightingale, and in her eyes was the unexpectant gaze of one who has ceased looking for coming gladness. When Joy sang, his voice soared upward as the lark's, and his step was the step of a conqueror who has never known defeat.

"But we can never be united," said Sorrow wistfully. Even as she spoke, they became conscious of a form standing behind them; dimly seen, but of a Kingly Presence. "I see him as the King of Joy," whispered Sorrow. "Before him, all my sorrow is melting away into deathless love and gladness." Said Joy softly, "But I see him as the King of Sorrow. The crown on his head is a crown of thorns, and the nailprints are the scars of a great agony."

"Then we are one in him," they cried in gladness, "for none but he could unite Joy and Sorrow." Hand in hand, they passed out into the world to follow him through storm and sunshine, in the bleakness of winter cold and the warmth of summer gladness . . . "as sorrowful, yet always rejoicing."

—*Mrs. Charles E. Cowman*

ARE THE SIMPLE CHOICES YOU'RE MAKING TODAY BUILDING A STEADY BASE OF TRUST AND OBEDIENCE UNDERNEATH YOU, SO THAT YOU CAN CONTINUE GROWING TOWARD A FULL LIFETIME OF FAITHFULNESS?

Elizabeth
SEEKING MOTHERHOOD

Selections from Luke 1

Wonder why God chose this "well along in years" woman to amaze with a miracle baby? We don't know if she had given up hope, or if perhaps she still prayed every day for the impossible. But we do know this— God can do anything with someone who seeks him.

There are some very human reasons for wanting a child. They draw attention like a magnet. Their little fingers and toes look like the dolls you always played with. And they're so cute in their costumes at the school play. But Elizabeth seems like a woman who had gotten beyond these kinds of desires. Her lifetime of faithfulness to the Lord indicates that her longing for a child came from a yearning to impart God's Word to a little one. And she certainly must have. John the Baptist's life was proof of powerful parenting.

Look At It This Way

When parents receive a child from the hand of God, their job, in the words of Janet Erskine Stuart, is "to give a saint to God." Who is sufficient for these things? This small package of living flesh, with their blood coursing through its tiny veins, their features alarmingly recognizable on the wizened face; real, workable fingers, capable of a damp, hot, strong grip on one of theirs; lungs which can produce the most heartbreakingly soft coos and unbearably harsh cries; skin so smooth, so silky, so tender you want to weep when you touch it. And they are responsible for this? Solely responsible—to give a saint back to God!

A talented woman was asked by a friend, "Why have you never written a book?"

"I am writing two," was the quiet reply. "I have been engaged in one for ten years, the other five. It doth yet appear what they shall be," said the woman, "but when he makes up my jewels, my great ambition is to find them there."

"Your children?"

"Yes, my two children. They are my life's work."

—*Elisabeth Elliot*

SOMETIMES IN THE HUBBUB OF BAND PRACTICE AND BALL GAMES, YOU CAN LOSE SIGHT OF THE PURPOSE OF MOTHERHOOD. PULL BACK THE FIRST CHANCE YOU GET, AND ASK GOD TO RENEW YOUR VISION.

Elizabeth

GENUINE LOVE

Selections from Luke 1

Mary was a maze of emotions on her hurried trek to Elizabeth's house. She was going with congratulations on her cousin's pregnancy. But to be honest, she needed someone to talk to. Elizabeth was one of those people who would really care.

Mary set out and hurried to a town in the hill country of Judah, where she entered Zachariah's house and greeted Elizabeth. When Elizabeth heard Mary's greeting, the baby leaped inside her, and Elizabeth was filled with the Holy Spirit.

Then she exclaimed with a loud cry: "Blessed are you among women, and blessed is your offspring! How could this happen to me, that the mother of my Lord should come to me? For you see, when the sound of your greeting reached my ears, the baby leaped for joy inside me! Blessed is she who has believed that what was spoken to her by the Lord will be fulfilled!"

*W*e Christians are actually pretty good at responding to a crisis, throwing our arms around a hurting friend, calling to check on someone who needs a listening ear. But too often when someone encounters a victory in her life, finds the man of her dreams, or takes a new job that doubles her salary, our congratulations are cloaked and guarded. It seems we're better at mourning with those who mourn than at rejoicing with those who rejoice. Does it take more strength to be the strong one . . . or the sincerely glad?

Look At It This Way

You are probably able to remember an occasion when someone greeted you in an outgoing and enthusiastic way which, surprisingly, made you uncomfortable. You realized something was wrong, but could not identify what it was. He was just being self-assertive and perhaps self-important.

I have also been greeted in another, quite different way. This person spoke to me as though he had been looking forward to meeting me, though I knew that couldn't be the case. He looked me carefully in the eyes, not glancing about to see who else was there to talk with. It was obvious that he was actually giving me his full attention, as though at this moment I was the most important person in the world.

We often find ourselves so preoccupied with our own concerns that we do not even see the people around us. We know they are there, but we do not see them as human beings God wants to love through us. Pray, "Lord, somebody important to you will touch my life today. Don't let me fail to be in touch with you and allow your love to be released through me."

—*Wayne McDill*

TRY GOING INTO A NEW DAY WITH YOUR EYES OPEN FOR THE PEOPLE YOU'LL ENCOUNTER AT THE STORE, THE OFFICE, THE SCHOOL OUTING, WHEREVER YOU'RE HEADED. GIVE SOMEONE YOUR FULL ATTENTION TODAY.

Anna
BEARING WITNESS

Selections from Luke 2

As she parades the infant Jesus around the temple like the proud grandmother she never got to be, she is doing what each of us is called to do— asking people to come closer, telling them what we've experienced, showing them how they can meet Jesus for themselves.

When the parents brought in the child Jesus to perform for Him what was customary under the law, Simeon took Him up in his arms. . . . There was also a prophetess, Anna, a daughter of Phanuel, of the tribe of Asher. She was well along in years, having lived with her husband seven years after her marriage, and was a widow for 84 years. She did not leave the temple complex, serving God night and day with fastings and prayers.

At that very moment, she came up and began to thank God and to speak about Him to all who were looking forward to the redemption of Jerusalem.

For many long, lonely years, Anna survived on the one thing that sets believers in Christ apart from all the other people of the world: hope. Hope based on a promise that God would send his Messiah to rescue his people from the bondage and oppression of sin. And still today, when you boil it all down, our message to the world—even to the world that comes disguised as our child's schoolteacher, our next-door neighbor, or our personal hair stylist—is hope. Hope beyond the slavery of sin. And hope beyond the grave.

Look At It This Way

Each person's story of how he encountered God provides another poignant illustration to those observing his life that God does exist. Just as the specific details of how I met my spouse describe to others how my life changed direction when I met someone significant, my description of knowing God is my record of our relationship. It is not a figment of my imagination, but an explanation of my encounter with someone who has changed my life.

I often have the opportunity to tell old friends and new acquaintances about my experiences with God. In fact, my faith is almost always well received when I simply share about my relationship with him. My personal experience is often more acceptable to an unbeliever or skeptic than any historical facts and evidences that I could rattle off.

When people share their experience of transformation, crediting the living, loving God with their visible, tangible change, this validates faith and allows others to hope, search, and find that God is powerful, present, and personal in our time.

—*Becky Tirabassi*

ARE YOU BEARING WITNESS FOR CHRIST? DOES YOUR TESTIMONY FLOW FREELY, NATURALLY? WHEN WILL YOU STOP WORRYING ABOUT WHAT OTHERS THINK—AND BE WORRIED ABOUT WHERE THEY'RE GOING?

Herodias
DISDAIN FOR GOD

Selections from Matthew 14

She may have been heartless before, but now she's got somebody to pin it on—someone who dares to declare that—(say this name slowly and sneeringly)—"Gahd" is not happy with her. Likely, she never changes her tune and dies in misery. Happy now, Herodias?

Herod had arrested John, chained him, and put him in prison on account of Herodias, his brother Philip's wife, because John had been telling him, "It's not lawful for you to have her!"...

When Herod's birthday celebration came, Herodias' daughter danced before them and pleased Herod. So he promised with an oath to give her whatever she might ask. And prompted by her mother, she answered, "Give me John the Baptist's head here on a platter!"... So he sent orders and had John beheaded in the prison. His head was brought on a platter and given to the girl, who carried it to her mother.

Surely you know someone who qualifies in your mind—and in the collective minds of your church friends or work associates—as an impossible sinner. A hopeless case. But if we're to stake our lives on the fact that God's grace is deep enough to drown even a giant-sized sin bucket into the sea of forgetfulness, then why do we run down any unsaved person in our conversation, or look over the top of our eyeglasses at the one who walks the aisle in our church? God is the only judge of that.

Look At It This Way

Right before the start of World War I, a French boy named Jean-Paul Sartre and his widowed mother were living with her parents—a Protestant and a lifelong French Catholic. By the time the war ended, Jean-Paul had grown thoroughly disenchanted with the church. He thoroughly hated to attend mass and resolved that he would go no more. To seal his decision, he stood before a mirror and cursed God. Three times he damned his Creator. He was through with God and the church.

Over the years, Sartre looked back at that event as a defining moment in his life. Shortly before his death, however, he relented, telling a journalist: "I do not feel that I am the product of chance, a speck of dust in the universe, but someone who was expected, prepared, prefigured—in short, a being whom only a Creator could put here." How tragic that Sartre allowed a decision in his youth to overshadow any consideration of God's relevance for nearly six decades. He spent most of his years embittered against others, struggling in vain for joy, meaning, peace, and strength.

—*Luis Palau*

GOD HAS BEEN KNOWN TO THROW THE WELCOME MAT OUT FOR PEOPLE WE'D NEVER BELIEVE COULD SUBMIT TO THAT KIND OF FREE GRACE. BUT BELIEF IS ALL THERE IS TO IT. DON'T YOU BELIEVE THAT?

The Canaanite Woman
PERSEVERING IN FAITH

What really takes more faith? To receive your answer to prayer the first time you ask? Or to keep coming back again and again, battling back your discouragement, ignoring your better judgment, never giving up hope that God will respond?

A Canaanite woman from that region came and kept crying out, "Have mercy on me, Lord, Son of David! My daughter is cruelly tormented by a demon." Yet He did not say a word to her. So His disciples approached Him and urged Him, "Send her away, because she cries out after us.". . . But she came, knelt before Him, and said, "Lord, help me!" He answered, "It isn't right to take the children's bread and throw it to their dogs."

"Yes, Lord," she said, "yet even the dogs eat the crumbs that fall from their masters' table!" Then Jesus replied to her, "Woman, your faith is great. Let it be done for you as you want."

Are you surprised at Jesus' first responses to the Canaanite woman—his cold answers to her impassioned pleas? Doesn't seem like the Jesus we know, does it? But how cold is it for a parent to make her child dig out the answer to a homework problem, or learn about the high cost of selfishness by letting him taste the consequences of his actions—not to make our kids squirm, but to force them to stretch their mental and moral muscles to new levels of strength. Shouldn't Jesus have the same concern for our faith?

Look At It This Way

O my heart, welcome all that is sent to prepare and to brace thee for a generous tomorrow. Welcome barrenness, snow and frost, limitations, frustrations, the strain of uncertainty, steep ways, dull ways. Welcome those things as the preparation for something made ready for thee before the foundations of the world.

Let thyself be broken. Let thyself be rent. Lay those keen yearnings in the hands that were wounded for thee. Let the winds blow, let the waves thunder; they cannot uproot the rock. Light, not darkness, is the ultimate conqueror. Not always shall our hearts cry out, *Lord, how long wilt Thou look upon this?* For sorrow and sighing shall flee away and the travail of the ages shall cease.

Cast not away, therefore, your confidence, which has great reward. He must reign. And he shall be as the light of the morning when the sun rises, even a morning without clouds, and the glorious majesty of the Lord shall endure forever. This assurance is among the things that cannot be shaken. So also is the peace that passeth all understanding.

—*Amy Carmichael*

FEEL LIKE YOUR PRAYERS ARE DISAPPEARING INTO THIN AIR— IGNORED AND UNANSWERED? PERSEVERE NO MATTER HOW POINTLESS THEY SEEM. YOU DON'T KNOW WHAT HE'S TOUGHENING YOU UP FOR.

Wife of Zebedee
PROMOTING HER CHILDREN

Selections from Matthew 20

She was just putting in a good word for her boys. It was a natural request. But do you see the tricky distinction between child-centered love and God-centered love? And how the natural love of the human heart can sometimes put us at odds with God's will?

The mother of Zebedee's sons approached [Jesus] with her sons. . . . "What do you want?" He asked her.

"Promise," she said to Him, "that these two sons of mine may sit, one on Your right and the other on Your left, in Your kingdom." But Jesus answered, "You don't know what you're asking. Are you able to drink the cup that I am about to drink?"

"We are able," they said to Him. He told them, "You will indeed drink My cup. But to sit at My right and left is not Mine to give; instead, it belongs to those for whom it has been prepared by My Father."

*M*others can often see other children as competitors. We tend to rate our own kids by how well they measure up against their classmates and cousins—sometimes being too hard on them for not making a better show, sometimes blinded to their flaws by our own favoritism. And it doesn't necessarily stop at school age but can continue into adulthood with the yardsticks of salary and success. But if God himself doesn't grade our children this way, then why should we—unless we're really grading ourselves?

Look At It This Way

There was policy by James and John in the management of this address, that they put their mother on to present it, that it might be looked upon as her request and not theirs. Though proud people think well of themselves, they would not be thought to do so. Therefore they affect nothing more than a show of humility, and others must be put on to court that honor for them which they are ashamed to court for themselves.

The mother of James and John was Salome (as appears by comparing Matthew 27:61 with Mark 15:40). Some think she was the daughter of Cleophas or Alpheus, and sister or cousin to Mary, the mother of our Lord. She was one of those women that attended Christ and ministered to him. They thought she had such an interest in him that he could deny her nothing, and therefore they made her their advocate.

It was their mother's weakness thus to become the tool of their ambition, which she should have given a check to. Those that are wise and good should not be seen in an ill-favored thing.

—*Matthew Henry*

ASK YOURSELF WHY YOU FEEL THE NEED TO PUSH YOUR CHILDREN OR TO MOTIVATE THEM TO EXCEL. MAKE SURE YOUR REASONS ARE HONORABLE AND GODLY, NOT SHORT-SIGHTED AND SELF-CENTERED.

Peter's Mother-in-Law
EAGER TO SAY THANKS

Selections from Mark 1

Lots of us will agonize in prayer over a particular need—its details never totally leaving the back of our minds— until God graciously answers. Then we close the curtain on this season of pleading by giving him a mere wave of thanks. Not this woman.

They went into Capernaum, and right away [Jesus] entered the synagogue on the Sabbath and began to teach. They were astonished at His teaching because, unlike the scribes, He was teaching them as one having authority. . . . His fame then spread throughout the entire vicinity of Galilee.

As soon as they left the synagogue, they went into Simon and Andrew's house with James and John. Simon's mother-in-law was lying in bed with a fever, and they told Him about her at once. So He went to her, took her by the hand, and raised her up. The fever left her, and she began to serve them.

Just as Peter's mother-in-law responded to her miraculously broken fever by putting dinner on the fire for Jesus and his disciples, we have regular opportunities to express our thanksgiving to God—not just by lavishing our praise toward the heavens, but by ministering to the needs of those around us. As much as God loves to hear our worship and adoration, surely he delights all the more in seeing our gratitude translated into simple kindnesses that keep the chain of praise unbroken, alive in others' hearts.

Look At It This Way

One reason why we don't thank God for his answer to our prayer is that frequently we don't recognize them as *being* answers to our prayers. We just take his bountiful supply or dramatic action for granted when it comes. This is why I teach my prayer seminar participants to jot down their prayer request, and then what happened, so they can put the two together.

Even worse, of course, is when God answers and we have forgotten that we even prayed. Keeping a list of our requests helps tremendously here. Then a periodic reading through the list of requests can be quite revealing: "Oh, yes, that provision, healing, or circumstance really was an answer to one of my prayers!" Then the thankfulness for it comes.

There are also those times when God deliberately waits long enough to answer so that there will be no doubt who gets the credit for what happens. It is only when I have exhausted all human resources that he finally answers—so that I will recognize the answer as coming from him. And thank him for it. And give him all the glory.

—*Evelyn Christenson*

HAVE YOU FORGOTTEN TO THANK GOD LATELY FOR HIS BOUNTIFUL BLESSINGS? WE COULDN'T LIVE WITHOUT EVEN THE SMALLEST OF HIS GIFTS. LET'S NOT MAKE HIM LIVE WITHOUT OUR HEARTFELT GRATITUDE.

Widow with Two Mites
GIVING ALL SHE HAD

Selections from Mark 12

The collection box had been rattling and clanging all morning with the treasures of earth, as the well-heeled received their "well dones" from the bystanding well-wishers. But when the poor widow deposited her meager tokens . . . well, Jesus said it had a heavenly ring.

Sitting across from the temple treasury, [Jesus] watched how the crowd dropped money into the treasury. Many rich people were putting in large sums.

And a poor widow came and dropped in two tiny coins worth very little.

Summoning His disciples, He said to them, "I assure you: This poor widow has put in more than all those giving to the temple treasury. For they all gave out of their surplus, but she out of her poverty has put in everything she possessed—all she had to live on."

*M*any of us have never given out of our lack. We often know that what's left over after our customary tithe is still enough to meet our needs—maybe not enough for pizza and a movie on Friday night or the most expensive ice cream at the store, but enough to keep genuine need at bay for another week. So if our giving only requires us to do without the unnecessary extras of life, does God really have the essential part of us—our absolute trust in him and our true love for others?

Look At It This Way

Shortly after my second child was born, I had just finished nursing school. My husband, Bruce, was still in college. And I didn't have a dress to wear for Sunday mornings. I remember looking at the money we had set aside for tithe and thinking it would do nicely for buying myself a dress. I remember God saying, "No," and my feeling guilty that I had even thought of it.

We went for a visit to my parents shortly after that time. While we were there, my dad told me to get ready because he was taking me to town. My dad, who hates to shop, and had never before bought me a dress, took me shopping for a dress. The fact that Dad gave it to me meant more than the dress ever could. That day, both of my Fathers had given me a dress. It was an act of love that I would have missed out on if I had bought the dress myself.

Are you a steward or owner of what God has given you—that which really still belongs to him? Show him your gratitude by giving first to him. He'll abundantly provide.

—*Penny Shoup*

THE CONTROL WE ALLOW GOD TO ASSUME OVER OUR MONEY IS A GOOD INDICATION OF HOW MUCH CONTROL HE HAS OVER THE REST OF US. MAKE SURE YOUR GIVING REFLECTS A GENUINE TRUST IN GOD'S SUPPLY.

Widow of Nain
DEALING WITH GRIEF

Selections from *Luke 12*

Her son was all she had left. Whatever flame still flickered on her trembling candle of hopes and dreams was now nothing more than a colorless trail of hollow smoke. Little did she know that where there's smoke, there's fire. And where there's God, there's hope.

[Jesus] was on His way to a town called Nain. His disciples and a large crowd were traveling with Him. Just as He neared the gate of the town, a dead man was being carried out. He was his mother's only son, and she was a widow. A large crowd from the city was also with her.

When the Lord saw her, He had compassion on her and said, "Don't cry." Then He came up and touched the open coffin, and the pallbearers stopped. And He said, "Young man, I tell you, get up!" The dead man sat up and began to speak, and Jesus gave him to his mother.

On the surface of your grief, it feels like you're pleading with God, raising your voice in order to get his attention. But he's long been aware of your need. Before the widow even knew that Jesus was anywhere in town, he had spotted her. He wasn't waiting to be asked. Before your heart has a chance to break, his has already gone out to you. Before your tears have begun their bitter journey, he has wept over you. Though you may not notice him, he's already there. Sitting right beside you. Giving you all you need.

Look At It This Way

Maybe God isn't trying to tell us anything specific each time we hurt. Pain and suffering are part and parcel of our planet, and Christians are not exempt. Suffering offers a general message of warning to all humanity that something is wrong with this planet and that we need radical outside intervention.

Another story from the Gospels may clarify this approach. In John 9, Jesus refutes the traditional explanation of suffering. His followers point to a man born blind. Clucking with pity, they ask, "Who sinned, this man or his parents?" The disciples wanted to look backward, to find out "Why?" Jesus redirected their attention. Consistently, he points forward, answering a different question: "To what end?"

And that, I believe, offers a neat summary of the Bible's approach to the problem of pain. To backward-looking questions of cause, to the "Why" questions, it gives no definite answer. But it does hold out hope for the future, that even suffering can be transformed or redeemed. Suffering offers an opportunity for us to display God's work.

—*Philip Yancey*

SEASONS OF GRIEF REVEAL WHERE WE'VE PLACED OUR HOPE. IF GOD IS ALL WE WANT IN THE EASY TIMES, HE'LL BE MORE THAN ENOUGH WHEN WE GET TO THE HARD ONES.

Woman Who Anointed Jesus
WELLING WITH WORSHIP

The sudden smell of perfume began breaking off conversations in mid-sentence, as the hum of the house slowly thinned into silence. What was she doing, this girl with her hair soaked in spikenard, tears streaming down her face? Didn't she know who Jesus was?

A woman in the town who was a sinner . . . brought an alabaster flask of fragrant oil and stood behind Him at His feet, weeping, and began to wash His feet with her tears. She wiped His feet with the hair of her head, kissing them and anointing them with the fragrant oil. . . .

Turning to the woman, He said to Simon, "Do you see this woman? I entered your house; you gave Me no water for My feet, but she, with her tears, has washed My feet and wiped them with her hair. . . . Therefore I tell you, her many sins have been forgiven; that's why she loved much.

Jesus introduces an interesting sidelight into this woman's worship—that the enormous measure of her forgiven sins inspired in her a greater measure of love. Perhaps you've never known a day when you doubted God. Maybe your testimony is so innocent and uneventful, it borders on boring. But you know deep down that your sin is as hideous as anyone's, and his grace is all that's holding you up. The place you started from may have made believing easy, but you've still got every reason to pour yourself out in worship.

Look At It This Way

One afternoon, my four-year-old and I were boisterously singing praise songs. We were clapping, raising our hands, and doing a variety of movements, when suddenly it struck me how free and uninhibited we were. We were giving our full selves unreservedly to God and raising up his name. Our hearts were open. Our true faces, unmasked, were upraised to him.

As we finished our medley, there was a tug at my heart. Was I always so free when worshiping God? Did I not often draw in, tone down, monitor, and dilute my praise, especially when worshiping with adults? And in those moments, was I not taking my eyes off the Lord and letting self creep back in? Had I not allowed insecurity, the need for acceptance and approval from others, and self-consciousness to steal my freedom and rob me—and those with whom I was worshiping—of the fullness of joy and the strength of unity that praising his name in worship brings?

It took singing with that sweet, open, four-year-old, who had no sense of self when worshiping God's name, to open my eyes.

—*Linda Atterbury*

WHAT'S HOLDING YOU BACK RIGHT NOW FROM LIFTING YOUR FACE UP TO GOD, CLOSING YOUR EYES, AND PRAISING HIM FROM THE BOTTOM OF YOUR HEART? STAY LONG ENOUGH TO MAKE SURE YOU MEAN IT.

Mary, Joanna, Susanna
FRIENDS OF JESUS

Selections from Luke 8

We're familiar with the apostles—the men Jesus hand-picked as his ministry helpers. But these women (and many others, the Scripture says) didn't wait to be asked. They willingly volunteered to serve and support their Savior—as many still do today.

Soon afterward [Jesus] was traveling from one town and village to another, preaching and telling the good news of the kingdom of God.

The Twelve were with Him, and also some women who had been healed of evil spirits and sicknesses: Mary, called Magdalene, from whom seven demons had come out; Joanna the wife of Chuza, Herod's steward; Susanna; and many others who were supporting them from their possessions.

The love and practical assistance that these women offered freely to the Lord certainly mark them as women of character. But Christ's willingness to receive help from them—especially when seen against the background of the times—reveals the depths of his love and the uniqueness of his ministry. A rabbi of that day was supposed to distance himself from women, not even allowed to speak to his own wife in public. Imagine the feathers Jesus ruffled by not only accepting a woman's help, but befriending her as well.

Look At It This Way

The recipe for every friendship must include one basic ingredient: agape love. It is an unconditional love. It is not based upon performance; it is given in spite of how the other person behaves. Agape love is also transparent love. It is strong enough to allow another person to know the real you.

Love means to commit yourself without guarantee, to give yourself completely in the hope that your love will produce love in the other person. Love is an act of faith, and whoever is of little faith is also of little love. Perfect love would be one that gives all and expects nothing. It would, of course, be willing and delighted to take anything that was offered, asking nothing in return. The person who expects nothing and asks nothing can never be deceived or disappointed.

Agape love is unique in that it causes us to seek to meet the needs of the other rather than demanding that our own be met. Our irritability and frustration diminish when we love another person because we are seeking to fulfill rather than be fulfilled. This is what agape is all about.

—Norman Wright

LIKE MANY OF THESE EXEMPLARY WOMEN, YOU MAY NOT FEEL LIKE YOU HAVE A LOT TO GIVE. BUT WILL YOU JOIN THEM IN GIVING WHAT YOU DO HAVE —OFFERING YOUR LIFE IN SERVICE TO THE KING?

Woman with Issue of Blood
GOING TO GOD

Selections from Luke 8

When her problem first surfaced, she went out hunting the doctor, but nothing he tried worked. So she resigned herself to just living with it —through the pain—until in the depths of desperation, she went out hunting for Jesus. And got the touch she needed.

A woman suffering from bleeding for 12 years, who had spent all she had on doctors yet could not be healed by any, approached from behind and touched the tassel of [Jesus'] robe. Instantly her bleeding stopped.

"Who touched Me?" Jesus asked. . . . When the woman saw that she was discovered, she came trembling and fell down before Him. In the presence of all the people, she declared the reason she had touched Him and how she was instantly cured.

"Daughter," He said to her, "your faith has made you well. Go in peace."

The truly amazing part of this story has always been Christ's awareness that healing power had flowed out of him at the woman's touch, that even with the impatient pushing and jostling of the pressing mob, he still maintained a sense of one-on-one attention. When will we realize that we're not troubling God with our questions and concerns? His heart is open to hear us—his touch nearer than our next thought—as if no one in the world existed but us. Our very personal God wants to hear from us personally.

Look At It This Way

My husband's paternal grandmother was a woman of prayer and unshakable faith. Her husband, father, and all of the men in her family were killed when Turks massacred the Armenians in the early 1900s. At the age of twenty-one, she was forced to flee with her two babies to Greece. Many years later, her daughter died of starvation.

Her only son was hundreds of miles away. When she was finally reunited with him, she found that he would have nothing to do with her simple faith. She watched as he became more and more entangled with sin and pride. She saw him succeed in every business he became involved with, but become more and more empty and miserable inside. She continued to pray.

Today, her son, her daughter-in-law, and all her grandchildren love the Lord. There is a little blue chair in the corner of their living room. No one sits on it. A new slipcover protects the old one, which is streaked and faded with her faithful, prayerful tears. It is there to remind all of us who have been affected by those prayers to never give up hope.

—*Gigi Graham Tchividjian*

MAYBE YOU'VE ALREADY TAKEN YOUR LATEST PROBLEM TO YOUR MOM, YOUR SISTER, OR THE FRIEND WHO TRADES OFF TAKING YOUR KIDS TO SCHOOL. BUT GOD HAS SOME ANSWERS OF HIS OWN. GO TO HIM.

Martha

DISQUIETED AND DISTRACTED

Selections from *Luke 10*

If you've ever had too much to do and not enough time to do it in . . . if you've ever scowled in the direction of people who were too spiritual for their own good . . . if you've ever done your work with a snippy attitude . . . Who are we kidding here? This story's for everybody!

While they were traveling, [Jesus] entered a village, and a woman named Martha welcomed Him into her home. She had a sister named Mary, who also sat at the Lord's feet and was listening to what He said.

But Martha was distracted by her many tasks, and she came up and asked, "Lord, don't You care that my sister has left me to serve alone? So tell her to give me a hand." The Lord answered her, "Martha, Martha, you are worried and upset about many things, but one thing is necessary. Mary has made the right choice, and it will not be taken away from her."

*I*f choosing to spend time alone with God is a real struggle—a heavy-handed demand that only adds more guilt and stress to your already overblown schedule—it's time to change the way you approach his presence. Faithful prayer warriors and devoted Bible lovers will tell you that their passion for disciplined quiet time with the Lord is not a sign of strength but an admission of weakness—a hard-earned realization that they are nothing on their own compared with who they are after they've been with him.

Look At It This Way

We must not compare ourselves to others, we Marys or Marthas, as we measure our own Christian hospitality. We need to affirm each other—whether we are Mary or Martha. In God's economy, we are all useful in the different forms of Christian hospitality.

As Mary undoubtedly shared some of the gems the Lord has spoken as she sat at his feet, I am sure Martha wished that she had stopped to listen a while and hear some of these treasures firsthand. Perhaps she thought, *Oh, I wish I had brought the apples in a bowl and sat at Jesus' feet, peeling and slicing them while he spoke.* And often I've wondered whether, if Mary had hurried to help Martha in the preparation and serving, there wouldn't have been plenty of time for both of them to sit at Jesus' feet and drink in his rich words of life.

In whatever area of Christian hospitality God has planned for us to serve, we need to claim the promises from his Word for our daily lives in order to have the strength and wisdom for every opportunity God sends our way.

—*Doris Greig*

YOUR KEY TO A MORE PRODUCTIVE DAY BEGINS WITH BEING DILIGENT TO SPEND TIME WITH GOD. WHEN HE COMES FIRST, EVERYTHING ELSE JUST SEEMS TO FALL INTO PLACE.

Martha
BELIEVING THE UNBELIEVABLE

Selections from John 11

Martha was trying so hard not to be upset with Jesus, even though it appeared he'd been too busy to help. She was trying hard not to be disillusioned with her faith, even though it wasn't seeming to help her right at the moment. Did he know how hard she was trying?

Martha said to Jesus, "Lord, if You had been here, my brother wouldn't have died. Yet even now I know that whatever You ask from God, God will give You."

"Your brother will rise again," Jesus told her. Martha said, "I know that he will rise again in the resurrection at the last day."

Jesus said to her, "I am the resurrection and the life. The one who believes in Me, even if he dies, will live. Everyone who lives and believes in Me will never die—ever. Do you believe this?"

"Yes, Lord," she told Him, "I believe You are the Messiah, the Son of God, who was to come into the world."

*J*ust when we think we've got everything figured out, something totally unexpected happens—something that we don't see how we're going to get through. *Why, God? Why?* No answer seems adequate. No formula can quite embrace it. But when we've asked every question, when we've searched every Scripture, when we've gone to everybody we know to see what they think and how they feel, we may be left with only Martha's answer: "I believe You are the Messiah." Can we let that answer be enough?

Look At It This Way

Not long ago, I sat with my daughter in the office of a specialist in orthopedic cancer. With misery in our hearts, we listened to his words. It seemed her leg must be amputated as soon as possible to keep the malignancy from spreading.

In the days that followed, I could not seem to find the inner strength I should have had as a Christian. My prayers were full of sobbing protests and petitions for my daughter's healing. As the two terrible weeks of waiting for the surgery passed, I finally began to realize that God was in control of this situation in which my hands were tied. He really did love my daughter, and his concern for her was even greater than mine. At last I was able to place my precious burden in his competent hands.

God had graciously used those painful weeks to show me a vacant area in my mind—an area containing knowledge, but lacking in that strong faith which comes from true wisdom. I realized that waiting on God was not just words, but an all-encompassing way of life.

—*Barbara Anderson*

WHAT PROBLEM IN YOUR LIFE IS BIGGER THAN YOUR ABILITY TO EXPLAIN? DON'T BE AFRAID TO BRING IT BEFORE GOD AGAIN. AND DON'T BE SURPRISED TO DISCOVER THAT YOU'LL JUST HAVE TO TRUST HIM.

Crippled Woman

FAITHFUL AND LONGSUFFERING

Eighteen years. Not just crippled, but imprisoned in a contorted position by a spirit—some supernatural force doing the devil's bidding— now set free by the healing power of Jesus Christ. And the Pharisees don't like it one bit. Well, that's their problem.

A woman was there who had been disabled by a spirit for over 18 years. She was bent over and could not straighten up at all. When Jesus saw her, He called out to her, "Woman, you are free of your disability."...

But the leader of the synagogue ... responded by telling the crowd, "There are six days when work should be done; therefore come on those days and be healed, and not on the Sabbath day." But the Lord answered him and said, "Hypocrites!... This woman, a daughter of Abraham, whom Satan has bound for 18 years— shouldn't she be untied from this bondage on the Sabbath day?"

We don't know if the synagogue was her customary place to be on the Sabbath. Might have been. Or perhaps she knew this Jesus fellow was going to be there that week—the one she'd heard could send the demons packing, could set the crippled free. Whatever the case, she was there. In church. Seeking help. Not curled up in a ball at home, resigned to her bed of pain. Somehow, she had limped her way to town that day. And caught his attention. And found her healing. He knows faith when he sees it.

Look At It This Way

Sometimes when I was a child, my mother or father would say, "Shut your eyes and hold out your hand." I trusted them, so whatever they were going to give me, I was ready to take. This is the way it should be in our trust of our heavenly Father. Faith is the willingness to receive whatever he wants to give, or the willingness not to have what he does not want to give.

From the greatest of all gifts (salvation in Christ) to the material blessings of any ordinary day (hot water, a pair of legs that work, a cup of coffee, a job to do and the strength to do it), every good gift comes down from the Father of Lights. Every one of them is to be received gladly and with thanks.

Sometimes we want things we were not meant to have. Because he loves us, the Father says no. Faith is willing not to have what God is not willing to give. Furthermore, faith does not insist on an explanation. It is enough to know his promise that he will give what is good—he knows so much more about that than we do.

—*Elisabeth Elliot*

YOU MAY HAVE SUFFERED LONG. BUT NEVER STOP GOING TO GOD FOR HELP—TO HOPE AND PRAY FOR HEALING, YES, BUT TO JUST BE HAPPY THAT HE KNOWS. AND CARES. AND WILL SEE YOU THROUGH.

The Woman at the Well
SHARING A NEW TESTIMONY

Selections from John 4

She was trying to just slip out quietly to the well that day, hoping not to run into anybody she knew —the same way you feel when you've hustled off on some quick errand with no make-up and your hair pulled back. But Jesus didn't pick up on her signals. Or did he?

A woman of Samaria came to draw water. "Give Me a drink," Jesus said to her.

"How is it that You, a Jew, ask for a drink from me, a Samaritan woman?" she asked. . . .

"Go call your husband," He told her, "and come back here."

"I don't have a husband," she answered. . . .

Jesus said, "For you've had five husbands, and the man you now have is not your husband.". . . Then the woman left her water jar, went into town, and told the men, "Come, see a man who told me everything I ever did!"

Before her hard veneer melted in Jesus' grace, the Samaritan woman attempted one of the classic dodges you'll meet in trying to share your faith with others—the doctrinal hot button. Her volley in verse 20 about orthodox worship sites has been replaced by topics such as fallen preachers, denominational differences, and general hypocrisy. But still, most of these maneuvers are just smoke screens that help lost people hide their needs and fears behind their clever opinions. Stick to your testimony. No one can argue with that.

Look At It This Way

This woman knew she was in trouble. Relationally, her life was a mess. I doubt she had many friends. She would have been mistrusted by women and joked about among men.

But Jesus looked at her—really looked at her—and talked to her as if she mattered, because to him, she did. Something about that gaze connected with her. She had no need to step out of her shadows into the sunlight of a stranger, but she revealed to Jesus that the man she was living with was not her husband.

What a gift Christ gave her in letting her know that he was aware of this and of all the rest as well. If he had offered her living water without ever revealing that he knew all the truth about her, perhaps she would have let his words of life bypass her, thinking, *If you only knew*. But he loved her enough to let her know, "I know it all, and I still love you." That unfamiliar and glorious gift changed her life so that, even as she was gulping it down, she was running to tell others the Good News.

—*Sheila Walsh*

PERPAPS THE GREATEST PIECE IN YOUR WITNESSING WARDROBE IS YOUR OWN STORY OF WHAT CHRIST HAS DONE FOR YOU. KEEP YOUR STORY IN GOOD ORDER. YOU NEVER KNOW WHEN YOU'LL NEED TO PULL IT OUT.

The Adulterous Woman
WITHIN REACH OF GRACE

Selections from John 8

You'll notice that this Bible passage is often set off with brackets and footnotes. It apparently doesn't appear in the earliest, most reliable manuscripts. But it's hard to deny the lessons that it teaches. It is so descriptive of Jesus. It is so descriptive of us.

"Teacher," they said to Him, "this woman was caught in the act of committing adultery."... When they persisted in questioning Him, He stood up and said to them, "The one without sin among you should be the first to throw a stone at her."...

When they heard this, they left one by one.... Only He was left, with the woman in the center. When Jesus stood up, He said to her, "Woman, where are they? Has no one condemned you?"

"No one, Lord," she answered.

"Neither do I condemn you," said Jesus. "Go, and from now on do not sin any more."

Be careful that your picture of Christ isn't cheapened by ignoring his final charge to the woman caught in adultery. Yes, his mercy is sweet, and it flows like living water into the darkest corners of our hearts—cleansing and purifying, healing and restoring. But not so we can excuse our bad habits or watch TV in a better mood. His undeserved grace should motivate us to put everything out on the table, to be watchful for hidden pockets of rebellion as he reveals them to us, and to slam the door on willful sin.

Look At It This Way

May the conviction of God come with swift and stern rebuke upon anyone who is remembering the past of others and deliberately choosing to forget their restoration through God's grace.

Certain forms of sin shock us far more than they shock God. The sin that shocks God is the thing that is highly esteemed among us—self-realization, pride, the right to myself.

We have no right to have the attitude toward any man or woman as if he or she had sunk to a lower level than those of us who have never been tempted on the line they have. We have to remember that in the sight of God there are no social conventions, and that external sins are not a bit worse in his sight than the pride that hates the rule of the Holy Spirit, though the life is morally clean.

May God have mercy on any one of us who forgets this and allows spiritual pride or superiority and a sense of our own unsulliedness to put a barrier between us and those whom God has lifted from depths of sin we cannot understand.

—*Oswald Chambers*

ARE THE PEOPLE IN YOUR LIFE WHO SEEM THE FARTHEST FROM GOD'S GRACE GETTING ANY CLOSER BY THE WAY YOU TALK ABOUT THEM, ACT AROUND THEM, PRAY FOR THEM? TRY SEEING THEM AS GOD DOES.

Mary Magdalene
NO LORD BUT CHRIST

Selections from John 20

Three days of mourning. A Sabbath spent in stunned, shaken silence. Now on Sunday, with eyes still red, her strength like water, she drags herself to the only place she knows to go—his grave. Just to be near him—to be near her Lord Jesus.

Mary stood outside facing the tomb, crying. . . . She saw two angels in white sitting there, one at the head and one at the feet, where Jesus' body had been lying. They said to her, "Woman, why are you crying?"

"Because they've taken away my Lord," she told them, "and I don't know where they've put Him.". . . She turned around and saw Jesus standing there, though she did not know it was Jesus. . . . Supposing He was the gardener, she replied, "Sir, if you've removed Him, tell me where you've put Him, and I will take Him away."

"Mary!" Jesus said.

The love of God is so vast, the power of his touch so invigorating, we could just stay in his presence for hours, soaking up his glory, basking in his blessings. But we can hear Jesus say across the ages, as he did to Mary in verse 17 of this passage: "Don't cling to me." It's not a rebuke but a reminder. Our times of close, uninterrupted fellowship with him are sweet—and necessary—but so are the times when we must turn our attention toward others, when we must take the reality of his love out into the world.

Look At It This Way

Mary of Magdala—the main witness mentioned at the Lord's tomb on Resurrection morning, the woman who lingered behind after the apostles' departure, the first person to greet Jesus after the Crucifixion—was commissioned by the Lord himself to carry the astounding announcement to his disciples. In all four Gospels, Mary is the only one placed at every scene related to Jesus' crucifixion and resurrection. Her faithful witness as the primary proclaimer of Jesus' message is not to be missed.

What an incredible testimony! Mary's story, so full of courage and commitment to God's Son, is worth remembering regularly. But let us also honor her for enduring the joyless agony of the Cross, staying with Joseph and Nicodemus as they wrapped the Lord's body, and keeping her tear-soaked watch at Jesus' tomb.

For Mary, God's grace of brokenness was part of the glory of that golden Resurrection morning. The gift of contrition cleared the way for Mary's faith to find its highest joy.

—*Debra Evans*

DOES JESUS SEEM FAR AWAY TODAY? DOES YOUR DEVOTION TIME SEEM MORE LIKE A DUTY THAN A DELIGHT? SEEK HIS FACE TODAY, AS MARY MAGDALENE DID, AND BE SATISFIED WITH NO OTHER.

Sapphira
ENSLAVED TO GREED

Selections from Acts 5

A man named Ananias, with Sapphira his wife, sold a piece of property. However, he kept back part of the proceeds with his wife's knowledge, and brought a portion of it and laid it at the apostles' feet. . . .

"Tell me," Peter asked her, "did you sell the field for this price?"

"Yes," she said, "for that price."

Then Peter said to her, "Why did you agree to test the Spirit of the Lord? Look! The feet of those who have buried your husband are at the door, and they will carry you out!" Instantly she dropped dead at his feet.

Some people will tell a lie when it's just as easy not to. Nobody would have found fault with this couple for keeping back some of the money for themselves from the sale of their land. But they wouldn't be caught dead looking chintzy, now would they?

Ananias and Sapphira's sin of greed came hand in hand with the sin of lying, which is often the case. But of all the lies our greed tempts us to make, the biggest lies are the ones we tell ourselves—the ones about how badly we need something, about what other people think about us, about how much we've suffered by doing without. It's easy to rationalize things when we're about to become the enriched recipients of our own buying decisions. But the joke's on us if we believe greed won't be back for more.

Look At It This Way

The most dangerous love affair any man or woman will ever experience in this life is a love affair with money. Money is a deceitful object of desire, because it can never deliver what it promises. It is no sin to be rich. But money is not neutral, and the individual who thinks so is only being foolish. If you have a love affair with money, you will never discover true riches, because you will never have them.

The great tragedy of materialism is that money can buy what seems to be happiness and what seems to be peace. What money does buy is pseudo-happiness and pseudo-peace, but it is not the real thing. Ask a sales professional who just closed the biggest deal of her life how long the thrill lasted. Ask a lottery winner how soon the high wore off. The pay-off is never what we think it will be. Real satisfaction is found more in the living and the doing than in the wealth.

Invest in what lasts. Souls last. God's kingdom lasts. Nothing else will. Investing in these will reap benefits not only now, but in eternity.

—*Ed Young*

TAKE A LOOK AROUND TODAY— THROUGH YOUR HOUSE, THROUGH YOUR CHECKBOOK, THROUGH YOUR LIFE. ARE YOU WILLING TO BE CONTENT WITH THE THINGS GOD HAS ALREADY BLESSED YOU WITH?

Tabitha
KNOWN FOR GOOD DEEDS

Selections from Acts 9

In Joppa there was a disciple named Tabitha. . . . She was always doing good works and acts of charity. In those days she became sick and died. . . . Since Lydda was near Joppa, the disciples heard that Peter was there and sent two men to him. . . .

When he arrived, they led him to the room upstairs. And all the widows approached him, weeping and showing him the robes and clothes that Dorcas had made while she was with them. Then Peter sent them all out of the room. He knelt down, prayed, and turning toward the body said, "Tabitha, get up!" She opened her eyes, saw Peter, and sat up.

Pressed between the pages of living legends like Peter and Paul is this remembrance of a little lady whose good name was won through her good works—little things that seemed rather unimpressive at the time. But look where her name is now.

Many people come to the end of their lives lonely, with no one to take an interest in them, now that they have nothing left to reciprocate with but endless demands and soiled bedpans. But rarely is that the case for those who have invested their lives in people. For them, the biblical principle of sowing and reaping begins wearing the face of loving children, grateful neighbors, and even long-forgotten strangers who'll never forget what that person did for them. Invest in people. It pays in ways you'd never expect.

Look At It This Way

There is no such thing as Christian work. That is, there is no work in the world which is, in and of itself, Christian. Christian work is any kind of work, from cleaning a sewer to preaching a sermon, that is done by a Christian and offered to God.

That means that nobody is excluded from serving God. It means that no work is beneath a Christian. It means there is no job in the world that needs to be boring or useless.

One of the results of the fall is that we lose sight of the meaning of things and begin to see the world as dull and opaque, instead of charged with glory. The job that is surely one of the world's pleasantest does not always hold much appeal to the one whose job it happens to be. It is difficult to keep in mind the spiritual character of our work (for there is spiritual character to all work that God gives us).

So let us lift up our work as a sacrifice, acceptable because it is lifted up to him who alone can purify.

—Elisabeth Elliot

IT DOESN'T REALLY TAKE THAT MUCH EFFORT TO GIVE SOMEONE ELSE'S NEEDS PRIORITY. YOU'D BE SURPRISED WHAT SIMPLE ACTS OF THOUGHTFULNESS YOU COULD COME UP WITH IF YOU'D THINK ABOUT IT FOR A MINUTE.

Lydia
DRAWN TO THE GOSPEL

Selections from Acts 16

One reason we shy away from sharing Christ is because we feel we can't hold our own intellectually, that we'd have to do a lot of convincing we're not prepared to do. But look at Lydia. Her heart was already open. So are a lot of other people's you know.

On the Sabbath day we went outside the city gate by the river, where we thought there was a place of prayer. We sat down and spoke to the women gathered there.

A woman named Lydia, a dealer in purple cloth from the city of Thyatira, who worshiped God, was listening. The Lord opened her heart to pay attention to what was spoken by Paul.

After she and her household were baptized, she urged us, "If you consider me a believer in the Lord, come and stay at my house." And she persuaded us.

Consider the premise that our whole life is wrapped up in this one act—that the full weight of our existence rests on simple trust in God's merciful gift of a life beyond this one. We make a thousand decisions a day, probably. Who knows how many in a lifetime? Yet only one is of supreme importance. If that one act of following Christ is all that stands between here and eternity for the people we know or meet, what should be Job One for us today? And what in the world are we waiting on?

Look At It This Way

"When your picture began appearing on all the trains and stations in London inviting me to 'bring my doubts' I decided to give it a shot—I had plenty of doubts to bring. As I sat and listened to you that night, you began to get through to me, and I started to get the disturbing feeling that some of what you said might be true. I went home and thought about it for several days and then sat down to write you a letter.

"I began to set out all my arguments as to why I didn't believe in Jesus Christ until, halfway through writing, I realized what I had written wasn't true. I did believe. So today, I sit writing a very different letter. You introduced me to Jesus, and I thank you from the bottom of my heart."

God isn't surprised when we struggle with unbelief. He isn't shocked when we rage against the evil and suffering all too frequently buffeting those we know and love. The question isn't, "Are there any valid arguments against God's relevance?" But, "Why am I afraid to consider the possibility of embracing relationship with him?"

—Luis Palau

GET YOURSELF READY TO BECOME A MORE FRUITFUL WITNESS BY PUTTING YOUR BELIEFS ON PAPER AND THINKING THROUGH YOUR BEST RESPONSES TO THE QUESTIONS OTHERS ARE LIKELY TO RAISE. BE PREPARED.

Rhoda
PLEASE BELIEVE ME

Selections from Acts 12

She was just a servant girl, but her story was an amazing one—that Peter the prisoner was now Peter on the porch. Really, we're just servants ourselves, trying to convince the world that the God of the Bible is also the Lover of their souls, the Forgiver of their sins.

Peter came to himself and said, "Now I know for certain that the Lord has sent His angel and rescued me.". . . When he realized this, he went to the house of Mary, the mother of John Mark, where many had assembled and were praying. He knocked at the door in the gateway, and a servant named Rhoda came to answer. She recognized Peter's voice, and because of her joy she did not open the gate, but ran in and announced that Peter was standing at the gateway.

"You're crazy!" they told her. But she kept insisting it was true. . . . When they opened the door and saw him, they were astounded.

*W*e need to always remember that the salvation story is a mystery. And even those of us who have embraced it didn't solve it on our own, but have had our hearts opened to it by the Holy Spirit. People are lost for many reasons—too busy to think about it, too confused by other belief systems, too hurt to believe God could really love them. Lots of reasons. It may take time before God melts their hearts to the warmth of his everlasting love. But like Rhoda, you just keep telling it till they can believe it.

Look At It This Way

In the corner of our simple den is a machine that represents just how far we've come in our ability to communicate with the world around us. This device looks like a regular telephone, but in fact it is one unit that has three incredible functions. With the touch of a few buttons, I can talk clearly to my mother some four hundred miles away. When I'm not home, this same machine will speak for me in my absence. Even more amazing, I can send a written message across the telephone wires, and it will be received on the other end without even wrinkling the paper.

Do I understand even a small part of this communication device? Absolutely not! But even though I have no earthly idea how it works, I know that it does.

The same is true when it comes to communicating effectively the message of Christ. Though I don't understand fully how this message of hope and redemption can change and transform a life, I just know it does. So the ultimate purpose of communication is to lift Christ up as the answer to all questions and needs.

—*Annie Chapman*

THE HARDEST ONES TO REACH WITH THE GOSPEL ARE OFTEN THE ONES IN YOUR OWN HOUSE, YOUR OWN FAMILY. WILL YOU KEEP PRAYING? AND KEEP TELLING THE STORY IN SPOKEN AND UNSPOKEN WAYS?

Priscilla
TEACHING THE WORD

Selections from Acts 18

Have you ever been guilty of telling someone what a great sermon you heard on Sunday, but when asked, you couldn't remember what it was even about? We live in a day of lazy thinking, where style determines substance. Be watching for the Word.

A Jew named Apollos, a native Alexandrian, an eloquent man who was powerful in the Scriptures, arrived in Ephesus. This man had been instructed in the way of the Lord; and being fervent in spirit, he spoke and taught the things about Jesus accurately, although he knew only John's baptism. . . .

After Priscilla and Aquila heard him, they took him home and explained the way of God to him more accurately. . . . After he arrived, he greatly helped those who had believed through grace. For he vigorously refuted the Jews in public, demonstrating through the Scriptures that Jesus is the Messiah.

The Bible tells us that Apollos was a very smart man—not just in the latest waves of Greek philosophy but in the Scriptures themselves. This was not someone flippantly handling his own half-baked theology. That's what makes his willingness to heed correction so amazing, because you'd think his natural response would have been to argue back. But this God-fearing couple apparently had a way of confronting a brother without either putting him down or turning him off. Grace and knowledge are a rare combination.

Look At It This Way

The Bible is a remarkable commentary on perspective. Through its divine message, we are brought face to face with issues and tests in daily living and how, by the power of the Holy Spirit, we are enabled to respond positively to them. Even in that timeless volume, we read about things that happen in our twentieth-century world. From its pages, we are instructed how to cope with or react to our modern problems in the proper perspective.

It addresses issues involving humility, waiting, suffering, self-centeredness, loss, adversity, prosperity, loneliness, fear . . . all of the things that get us down. Without this perspective, we make ourselves (and everybody else) miserable because we think we are the apex upon which the world turns. We think the sun rises and sets in our coming and going. Generally, when we live out our lives in that cocoon, we are not only a disappointment and a trial to be with, but we are impoverished and ineffectual as well. The proper perspective creates within us a spirit of reaching outside of ourselves with joy and enthusiasm.

—Luci Swindoll

YOU MAY NEVER BECOME ONE OF THOSE PEOPLE WHO CAN QUOTE CHAPTER AND VERSE ON ANY SUBJECT. BUT HOW CAN YOU REALLY KNOW WHAT YOU BELIEVE UNLESS YOU KNOW WHAT THE BIBLE SAYS?

Phoebe
NOTEWORTHY SERVICE

Phoebe's tribute is short and simple—"She has been a benefactor of many." It's surely the understatement of a long-ago year. But knowing women like Phoebe, I'm sure she treated these words as a lot of fuss about nothing. Shucks, she was just glad she could help.

I commend to you our sister Phoebe, who is a servant of the church in Cenchreae. So you should welcome her in the Lord in a manner worthy of the saints, and assist her in whatever matter she may require your help. For indeed she has been a benefactor of many—and of me also. . . .

Now I implore you, brothers, watch out for those who cause dissensions and pitfalls contrary to the doctrine you have learned. Avoid them; for such people do not serve our Lord Christ but their own appetites, and by smooth talk and flattering words they deceive the hearts of the unsuspecting.

Phoebe's name literally means *bright*. And those who serve like her brighten the lives of others in ways that few ever see, but which extend God's blessings to many—to their churches, neighbors, and families—to the sick, the imprisoned, the dying—to the weary, the lonely, the downcast. The thanks you receive may (like Phoebe's) be brief and infrequent, but keep letting your light shine, "so that they may see your good works and give glory to your Father in heaven." (Matthew 5:16). What more thanks could you want?

Look At It This Way

God calls us to present-moment service. This takes constant awareness of who we're with or what we're doing at the present moment. Who does God want me to help or to speak to now? What hard or easy task can I do for his glory?

Present-moment service doesn't replace a ministry we're already doing. It means that we remain open to surprise opportunities to share the Lord while we're serving. Rather than being totally focused on the service we're doing and what we've determined to accomplish, we listen for the Holy Spirit's guidance about what he would have us do this minute. This is where wisdom and spiritual discernment are so vital . . . knowing when to say yes or no to what we're asked to do.

God calls us to seek him daily in order to serve him daily. Through our devotional time and as we constantly carry on a conversation with the Lord and listen for his still, small voice throughout the day, we'll become more and more tuned to what he desires for us. We'll know how to lovingly serve others as we trust him to give us the guidance we need.

—*Sheila Cragg*

YOUR DATEBOOK IS ALREADY FILLED TO OVERFLOWING. BUT HOW MANY OF THOSE ACTIVITIES ARE DESIGNED TO SERVE, TO GIVE, TO POUR OUT GOD'S BLESSING ON OTHERS? ARE YOU MAKING TIME TO BE A LIGHT?

Wife of an Unbeliever
STAYING TRUE

Selections from 1 Corinthians 7

Hang in there. That's the Bible's simply stated, yet understandably difficult advice for wives whose husbands don't yet share their eternal destiny. The Spirit can accomplish amazing turnarounds. Are you prepared to be the tool he probably uses the most?

If any woman has an unbelieving husband, and he is willing to live with her, she must not leave her husband. For the unbelieving husband is sanctified by the wife. . . . But if the unbeliever leaves, let him leave. A brother or a sister is not bound in such cases. God has called you to peace.

For you, wife, how do you know whether you will save your husband? Or you, husband, how do you know whether you will save your wife? However, each one must live his life in the situation the Lord assigned when God called him. This is what I command in all the churches.

*I*f you already have a Christian husband, how are you and he working together to uplift and encourage each other? What boundaries or accountability measures do you have in place in your home to ensure that each of you has an extra set of eyes watching out for them? How committed are you to breaking the ice of prayerlessness so that you and your mate can seek the Lord openly and honestly together, releasing control over your marriage into the capable, trustworthy, but often surprising hands of God?

Look At It This Way

The hard part about being a praying wife is maintaining a pure heart. If you have resentment, anger, unforgiveness, or an ungodly attitude—even if there's good reason for it—you'll have a difficult time seeing answers to your prayers. But if you can release those feelings to God in total honesty, there is nothing that can change a marriage more dramatically.

I wish I could say that I've been regularly praying for my husband from the beginning of our marriage until now. I haven't. Oh, I prayed. The prayers were short: "Protect him, Lord." They were to the point: "Save our marriage." But most commonly, they were my favorite three-word prayer: "Change him, Lord."

Gradually I realized that it's impossible to truly give yourself in prayer for your husband without first examining your own heart. I couldn't go to God and expect answers to prayer if I harbored unforgiveness, bitterness, or resentment. I couldn't pray my favorite three-word prayer without knowing in the deepest recesses of my soul that I had to first pray *God's* favorite three-word prayer: "Change *me*, Lord."

—*Stormie Omartian*

IF YOUR HUSBAND IS UNSAVED, FORCE YOURSELF TO PRAY UNTIL YOU CAN BELIEVE WHAT YOU'RE ASKING FOR. AND PRAY FOR A FRIEND TO COME ALONGSIDE YOU TO ADD UNITED STRENGTH TO YOUR REQUESTS.

Women Worshiping
EXERCISING FREEDOM WISELY

Selections from 1 Corinthians 11

This is a tough passage to deal with, because it was obviously written to address a cultural issue which first-century Christians would have readily understood. But is there a lesson we're supposed to learn from it? Yes—the careful use of Christian freedom.

> *Every woman who prays or prophesies with her head uncovered dishonors her head, since that is one and the same as having her head shaved.*
>
> *A man, in fact, should not cover his head, because he is God's image and glory, but woman is man's glory. For man did not come from woman, but woman came from man; and man was not created for woman, but woman for man. . . .*
>
> *Does not even nature itself teach you that if a man has long hair it is a disgrace to him, but that if a woman has long hair, it is her glory? For her hair is given to her as a covering.*

This is a classic case of Romans 14 maturity: "For none of us lives to himself, and no one dies to himself. . . . Instead decide not to put a stumbling block or pitfall in your brother's way. . . . Pursue what promotes peace and what builds up one another" (vv. 7, 13, 19). The development of the new believer and the precious price of the unredeemed soul should always override our desire to exercise a freedom that we know will raise unnecessary eyebrows and could perhaps be costly to the cause of Christ.

Look At It This Way

The Corinthians' freedom manifested itself in various ways in the worship life of the church. One way was a push by the women of the church for equality with men. The women were removing the symbol of their subordination and the mark of their modesty—their veils—and participating with bare heads in the exhorting and praying in the worship services. Their belief that they were experiencing now the life of the kingdom of God, in which sex distinctions would no longer exist, emboldened the women to act out the freedom they had been promised as Christians.

But Paul saw in the laying aside of the veil a threat to God-established order and possibly to the morals and reputation of the church. Women of good character covered their heads in public; prostitutes did not. Paul would be quite willing to grant that when the kingdom of God actually comes in glory and not simply in anticipation, all distinctions of rank and sex will vanish. But the great day has not yet come. Meanwhile, we must maintain appropriate social structures and conventions.

—*Edward P. Blair*

THE WEARING OF A VEIL ON OUR HEADS ISN'T A BURNING ISSUE IN TODAY'S CHURCH OR CULTURE. BUT ARE THERE OTHER MATTERS OF MODERN-DAY CLOUT THAT DESERVE THE WEIGHT OF OUR CONSIDERATION?

Euodia & Syntyche
QUIBBLING & QUARRELING

Selections from Philippians 4

If these two's squabble was like some of ours, they'd probably have a hard time remembering what started it. But an unwise word was spoken, an unkind thought became a harsh reaction —one thing just sort of led to another, and before you knew it . . .

I urge Euodia and I urge Syntyche to agree in the Lord. Yes, I also ask you, true partner, to help these women who have contended for the gospel at my side, along with Clement and the rest of my co-workers whose names are in the book of life.

Rejoice in the Lord always. I will say it again: Rejoice! Let your graciousness be known to everyone. The Lord is near. Don't worry about anything, but in everything, through prayer and petition with thanksgiving, let your requests be made known to God. And the peace of God, which surpasses every thought, will guard your hearts and your minds in Christ Jesus.

Have you ever considered what quarreling really costs—in our marriage, our family, our workplace, our church, our circle of friends? First, it costs us all that wasted time and energy spent pretending we're telling someone off while we're driving or doing the dishes. It costs us the freedom of not having someone to avoid or to hope doesn't call. It costs us the satisfaction of having no regrets for the things we've said in anger. And it costs us clear fellowship with God. Disagreements happen. But brave people stop them.

Look At It This Way

SYNTYCHE (to Lydia): Have you read that part of the letter to her?

EUODIA: What part? Does it say something about me?

SYNTYCHE: *Us*, Euodia. Paul addresses *us*—by name.

LYDIA (unrolls letter): "I entreat Euodia and I entreat Syntyche to agree in the Lord."

EUODIA: He knows about us? Who told him? Why bother Paul with such a trivial little thing as . . .

SYNTYCHE: Probably because it's not a trivial little disagreement anymore. Probably because it's gotten to the point that it's begun to hurt the church—and to hurt the cause of Christ.

EUODIA: But . . . but I never intended to . . .

LYDIA: Of course not, Euodia, but it has.

EUODIA: But how can we agree? We *don't* agree! About *anything!*

LYDIA (reading letter): I don't think he's asking you to agree about everything. I mean, if God wanted us to agree all the time, why did he make us all so different? But I think Paul means that in our Lord Jesus Christ, all of us can meet. None of us has an exclusive right to claim him, for he came to save us all.

—*Robert Don Hughes*

ARE YOU QUARRELING WITH SOMEONE RIGHT NOW? IS THERE SOMETHING UNSETTLED OR UNSPOKEN BETWEEN YOU AND ANOTHER THAT COULD PERHAPS START TO CLEAR WITH ONE FORGIVING WORD FROM YOU?

The Christian Widow
MOVING ON

Selections from 1 Timothy 5

It's comforting to know that whatever we face in life, many more have already felt the same pain and asked the same questions. But even more comforting is knowing that God has left no one out of his plan. His Word reveals his love for us in every season of life.

Support widows who are genuinely widows. But if any widow has children or grandchildren, they should learn to practice their religion toward their own family first and to repay their parents, for this pleases God. The real widow, left all alone, has put her hope in God and continues night and day in her petitions and prayers; however, she who is self-indulgent is dead even while she lives. Command this, so that they won't be blamed.

Now if anyone does not provide for his own relatives, and especially for his household, he has denied the faith and is worse than an unbeliever.

When you're young, and the thought of death sneaks into a mind crowded with places to go and people to meet, you wonder how anybody faces up to it. But when death has already found its way to your house, you start to be less afraid of its frightening glare. You still consider life a gift from God, but there's a gleam of grace in death's eye you never saw before—not a morbid longing to die but a freedom to live unafraid of its shadow, because the treasure that awaits you—reuniting with your lifelong mate—just got more valuable.

Look At It This Way

When a woman loses her husband, God then makes a personal commitment to protect her himself. It is a comforting, beautiful assurance to know that an omnipresent, omnipotent, omniscient God is watching tenderly over the widow, providing for her physical needs, guarding against dangers to her, and faithfully directing her life.

"The LORD . . . keeps the widow's boundaries intact" (Proverbs 15:25, NIV). This verse is an awesome testimony to the responsibility the Lord accepts concerning the widow. It is as if God places an invisible wall around the widow.

But how can a widow secure this divine protection and special blessing? The widow who wants his protective care must consecrate or set herself apart to the Lord. Through her own faith and commitment, she steps within the boundaries of God's protective area. This commitment to the Lord moves her away from vulnerability to Satan's favorite assault against widows (self-pity, idleness, uselessness, and despair) and opens her to a new assignment from God in ministry.

—*Dorothy Kelley Patterson*

NO ONE CAN KNOW THE DEPTHS OF A WIDOW'S SORROW. BUT WHATEVER HEARTACHE WE OFFER UP TO GOD, HE WILL TEMPER IT WITH USEFULNESS AND MAKE US A BLESSING BEYOND OUR YEARS.

Lois & Eunice
PASSING DOWN THE FAITH

Selections from 2 Timothy 1

We don't know anything else about these women of God except what you're about to read. But the Bible does give us a rather lengthy look at their son and grandson. So in a way, we know a lot about them. Aren't our children our most telling reflection?

To Timothy, my dearly loved child. . . . I thank God, whom I serve with a clear conscience as my forefathers did, when I constantly remember you in my prayers night and day. Remembering your tears, I long to see you so that I may be filled with joy, clearly recalling your sincere faith that first lived in your grandmother Lois, then in your mother Eunice, and that I am convinced is in you also.

Therefore, I remind you to keep ablaze the gift of God that is in you through the laying on of my hands. For God has not given us a spirit of fearfulness, but one of power, love, and sound judgment.

There was a day when the generations weren't so far apart—when Grandma used to live next door or in the extra bedroom upstairs, not three states and seven hundred miles away. It means that for many of us, staying close to our children and grandchildren, taking seriously the task of imparting to them our years of firsthand Christian experience, requires a lot more time and effort. This might be a good week to start dropping some letters of memory and encouragement in the mail. Then you won't seem so far away.

Look At It This Way

One of the most precious responsibilities of grandparents is the sharing of faith from generation to generation. There has often been a special bond between grandparents and grandchildren—a bond of love and affection which opens communication in a unique and penetrating manner. Grandparents are honored for their years of wisdom and needed for their loving sensitivity. They have the privilege of reinforcing the godly lessons taught by parents and supplementing the spiritual nurture of the younger generation.

Parents, too, are recipients of the benefits of grandparenting. They have access to counsel based upon their years of knowledge and experience. They receive cooperation and encouragement as they feel the awesome demands of parenthood, and they can find some coaching and tutoring available for the asking.

Parenting is a lifetime pursuit, and it only becomes "grander" when extended over the generations. If we could call back to active duty the grandparents of the world, wouldn't it make a difference in the next generation?

—*Dorothy Kelley Patterson*

IF YOU DO NOTHING ELSE IN THIS LIFE BUT HELP TO KEEP THE SACREDNESS OF CHRISTIAN FAITH ALIVE INTO THE NEXT GENERATION, YOU WILL HAVE SUCCEEDED. RECOMMIT YOURSELF TO THAT TASK TODAY.

Mentoring Women
PASSING THE TORCH

Selections from Titus 2

Why should today's young people have to learn their lessons the hard way, when we've already walked so many of the same pathways, felt so many of the same pressures, seen so many of the Lord's promises come true? So many of them need us so much.

Older women are to be reverent in behavior, not slanderers, not addicted to much wine. They are to teach what is good, so that they may encourage the young women to love their husbands and children, to be sensible, pure, good homemakers, and submissive to their husbands, so that God's message will not be slandered. . . .

For the grace of God has appeared, with salvation for all people, instructing us to deny godlessness and worldly lusts and to live in a sensible, righteous, and godly way in the present age, while we wait for the blessed hope and the appearing of the glory of our great God and Savior, Jesus Christ.

Few of us really think we have a lot to say to others. Our lives—because they're ours, the only eyes we've ever looked through—can seem quite ordinary, uneventful, unimportant. But we have something we can share—things no one else has seen quite the way we've seen them. Even our fears and failures—even the ones we struggle with at this very moment—are object lessons that have much to teach, to reveal, to inspire. We can't do everything, but can we do anything more valuable than invest ourselves in another?

Look At It This Way

My dear "Mom Cunningham" schooled me—not in a class or seminar, or even primarily by her words. It was what she *was* that taught me. It was her availability to God. It was the surrender of her time. It was her readiness to get involved, to lay down her life for one anxious Bible school girl. Above all, she herself, a simple Scottish woman, was the message.

Think of the vast number of older women today. We live longer now than we did forty years ago. There is more mobility, more money around, more leisure, more health and strength—resources which, if put at God's disposal, might bless younger women. But there are also many more ways to spend those resources, so we find it very easy to occupy ourselves selfishly.

Where are the women, single or married, willing to hear God's call to spiritual motherhood, taking spiritual daughters under their wings to school them as Mom Cunningham did me? She had no training the world would recognize. She simply loved God and was willing to be broken bread and poured-out wine for his sake. Retirement never crossed her mind.

—Elisabeth Elliot

CAN YOU IMAGINE WHAT WOULD HAPPEN IF EACH OF US FOUND SOME TEENAGERS IN OUR CHURCHES, SCHOOLS, OR NEIGHBOR-HOODS, AND BEGAN OPENING OUR HEARTS TO THEM IN GODLY DISCIPLESHIP?

Sources

Sources

Sources

If you liked this book, there are plenty more
One Minute Bible™ devotional collections:

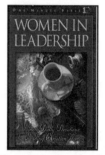

Women in Leadership
0-8054-9193-7

Men in Leadership
0-8054-9153-8

90 Days with the
Christian Classics
0-8054-9278-X

90 Days in the Word for
Business Professionals
0-8054-9363-8

Starting Today
0-8054-3780-0

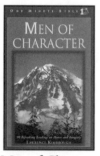

Men of Character
0-8054-2685-X